LEARNING UNSCRIPTED

Simon Birt

Presentations & Conversations
with
Learning Leaders

Equinox PH also publishes its books in a variety of electronic formats and by print-on-demand. Some material included with standard print versions of this book may not be included in e-books or print-on-demand.

Cover graphic by: Vivienne McDougall
Cover design by: Vivienne McDougall
Page design by: Vivienne McDougall

In publication data:
Birt, Simon.
    Learning Unscripted: Presentations and Conversations with Learning Leaders / by Simon Birt; first edition.
    Pages 241

ISBN-10: 0986166219
ISBN-13: 978-0986166211

1.--Technology Enhanced Learning. 2.--Social Business Strategy & Implementation. 3.--. Strategic Thinking. 4..--Global Sales & Integrations. 5. --E-Learning.. 6. --Mobile Learning. 7..--Social Learning. 8..--Cloud Technology. 9..-- Business Value Creation. 10.-- Learning Planning. 11..--Ideas & Innovation for Creative Training. 12.--Content Authoring. 13. ---Gamification & Game-based Learning .

FIRST EDITION

ABOUT THE BOOK

In 'Learning Unscripted', Simon Birt shares enlightening conversations with global experts from organizations such as IBM, PepsiCo, the NHS, and the Walt Disney Corporation about their learning technologies and training methods. He also offers some of his own insights and knowledge through friendly, informal, and easy-to-understand presentations.

Covering topics such as E-Learning, Mobile Learning, Social Learning, Gamification, Content Authoring, 70:20:10, the Use of Cloud Technology to Support Learning, Business Value Creation, Learning Planning, Ideas & Innovation for Creative Training, and more, 'Learning Unscripted' offers a wealth of ideas for both theory and practice.

For those wishing to familiarize themselves with the key topics of contemporary organizational learning, whether novice or L&D professional, 'Learning Unscripted' has something for everyone.

www.simonbirt.org

@sblearntech

uk.linkedin.com/in/simonbirt

simon@simonbirt.org

http://bit.ly/1FYzyss

ABOUT THE AUTHOR

Simon Birt is a thought-leader and expert in TEL (Technology Enhanced Learning), Social Business Strategy & Implementation, Strategic Thinking and Global IT Integrations. He works with organizations on the correct applications of learning as delivered by the three key channels of Social, Mobile and Cloud, as well as the use of these channels to support Formal and Informal Learning. Birt also has a broad perspective of the ways in which effective learning and training can impact overall efficiency, sales and performance.

After an early career as a commissioned officer with the Royal Marine Commandos (UK), Simon Birt has spent the last 20 years working for and with some of the world's most influential technology companies such as Oracle, IBM, Swisscom and Trivantis. He has held several top corporate positions. Birt also acts as a Strategic Consultant on TEL to large organizations such as the European Commission..

Simon Birt is based in Europe and the United States. He travels extensively to present his ideas at key exhibitions and conferences worldwide, and also works with organizations on contemporary learning and development strategies.

CONTENTS

CONTENTS

CHAPTER 1

INTRODUCTION

The Learning and Development Industry is a fast changing one. When I first started working in it in 2007 (having been in a succession of software and technology companies in my career), it struck me that L&D didn't appear to be like other sectors I knew. It was tremendously fractured, populated by people who seemed to be academic in form but business-like in nature.

The Learning Industry is full of theories, ideas, and research-led teaching models rubbing shoulders with profitability and business-value creation.

Mixing the worlds of learning and profit-making is bound to create friction, and so it does. Too often business people don't see the real value of learning and training programs, and Learning and Development (L&D) professionals increasingly have to justify and measure learning and training value, even though it just seems logical that well-trained employees perform better than those who aren't. Which is true. But, like many areas of business, measurement not only provides the basis for justification, it also provides insight.

I started venturing out to learning exhibitions and trade-shows shortly after starting in the industry and realized what a unique sector it is. Here one finds academics from schools and universities from all over the world mixing with corporate professionals going to the same presentations on E-Learning, web classrooms, Learning Management Systems, Mobile Learning, etc. In the middle lie the software vendors selling their products and doing a super job of fulfilling the demand. The Learning and Development market is a mighty 50+billion dollar market annually.

Accountability and business value are intrinsically tied to learning and development today. Measurement and justification are always right behind the latest training and learning models to emerge in the corporate world. Rightly so. One could argue that, in the past, a lack of good measurement has seen many good learning programs falter and close down before their value was entirely realized, all for the lack of proper data linked to said business value. Bringing understanding of how much a certain learning exercise has impacted the bottom line is a vital piece of the L&D role now. For the academic and business worlds to exist in harmony, this is critical.

In this book, I have transcribed the presentations and conversations which formed a series of webinars I recently presented on the internet. I had interviews with several people who are leaders in learning, and who are in the middle of this struggle between academic exercise and business profitability. They have all enthusiastically embarked upon untried and unproven methods to bring better learning experiences to employees. They can equally point to success. The merit lies in what they have managed to achieve using the resources available to them.

Whether it is Lee Kitchen talking about trying out innovation and problem-solving methods to get business leaders at Disney to do unusual things, or Charles Jennings working tirelessly to promote his approach to 70:20:10 Learning with corporations such as Shell, Reuters, or Philips, all my interviewees have been through trial-and-error experiences. Today they have solid foundations and all the supporting evidence that what they believed in is justified and works well. Intermingled with these interviews are presentations that I have made about learning topics that occupy the world of learning and development today. I hope you enjoy the mixture and the insightful wisdom of my guests in this book.

Simon Birt

CHAPTER 2

E-LEARNING,

MOBILE LEARNING,

AND

SOCIAL LEARNING

WITH

SIMON BIRT

The way we use content for learning is changing. New technologies are developing quickly. In this session I cover the three main types of content we see emerging in our industry. I also cover how we should think about the use and creation of this content, and how to distribute it to generate positive learning activity and collaboration.

Let's examine the content with regards to these three key areas: E-Learning, Mobile Learning and Social Learning. These are the three most active areas for distance learning content today.

DEFINITIONS AND CHARACTERISTICS OF THE CONTENT TYPES

In this section, I will highlight some of the differences I see between these types of content.

First of all, let's look at E-Learning itself. I'm going to go through each of these three areas in detail to point out the key aspects of each one as we go forward.

E-LEARNING

Definition:

E-Learning is training delivered as digital content, which learners work through from computers, often at a distance, in their own offices or homes. E-Learning consists of formal content and is hosted on a Learning Management System, which the learner accesses via a browser, and which tracks and stores the learner's results.

KEY POINT – E-Learning is developed and produced by the Training or Learning and Development (L&D) department.

First of all, E-Learning is typically developed by a training or L&D department. It's something that these departments take ownership of. This allows for control of standards, production to a high and consistent level, and moderation of the information used. In some industries it is critical to ensure that content complies with regulation and teaches the correct knowledge, sometimes with an audit process included.

KEY POINT – E-Learning takes time to develop and complete.

E-Learning content takes time to develop. According to the American Association for Talent Development (ATD formerly ASTD) estimates, one hour of E-Learning content will take anything from 50 to 300 hours of *development* time depending on the complexity of the content (content using only text being nearer the 50 hours, for example, and content using video with a high level of interactivity taking nearer 300 hours). This is a guide and other factors will affect the development time. (This does not include time taken for the Business Process where story-boarding, approvals and review of the content will include delays. See below.)

The point is that it takes time to storyboard and create good E-Learning content. E-Learning follows a design process such as **ADDIE**, (Analysis, Design, Development, Implementation and Evaluation), around which Instructional Designers centralize their project.

Normally there are quite a few people involved in the creation process. It takes additional time to complete because of this. The content is developed from a storyboard, often involving Clients,

Developers and Instructional Designers and a lengthy development, review and approval process. It also involves tests and trainers, so a sizable amount of professionals and experts are involved.

KEY POINT – E-Learning is often of high quality development and production with use of professional video, graphic design, animations, interactivity, storyboards, Gamification, and testing. E-Learning content has high-quality, professional production. Very often it employs professional video, graphics and animations, and is built for the standardized training of many employees. The content is created to a standard so that it remains consistent.

As a consequence, new technologies are being explored. Today we see Gamification (see chapter 8) and Virtual Reality emerging as exciting areas for development.

KEY POINT – E-Learning has high production costs, employs in-house and outsourced content development, and bought-in content is common.
Consequently, E-Learning comes with quite high production costs. Despite becoming more and more competitive in today's market,

good quality interactive learning content comes at a price. Often, it is in-house developed and/or outsourced content. However, it is noticeable that there's a trend in larger organizations to bring this in-house more and more. Bought-in content is quite common. So you see companies that specialize in creating content of a standard nature, such as computer training courses, license their content for access via subscription. That's an example of what I referred to as 'bought-in content'.

KEY POINT – E-Learning follows standards.

Typically, E-Learning content follows standards such as **SCORM** (Shareable Content Object Reference Model) which allows E-Learning content to be played in a common format across different types of LMS. It follows **508 compliance,** which is a federal law mandating that all electronic and information technology developed, procured, maintained, or used by the federal government be accessible to people with disabilities. And finally, **AICC** (Aviation Industry CBT Committee), which is compliance with one of nine AICC Guidelines and Recommendations (AGRs). We have, therefore, got some standards to think about with E-Learning content development.

KEY POINT – E-Learning is used for formal training and compliance.

I'm now going to talk about what we use E-Learning for. It doesn't suit all learning activities, but for some it is very useful. For example, E-Learning is well-suited to those training needs requiring certification and compliance.

Many organizations have requirements for certification and/or compliance. These requirements often demand that employees follow very formalized training processes. We've adapted E-Learning to help us address these particular requirements very well. It has saved us a lot of money in doing so because it's allowed us to do our training online. It's allowed us to move away from the classroom, which can be expensive and disruptive to business. On the whole, this has been a very positive step for training.

KEY POINT – E-Learning demands learner focus, a quiet place and user interaction.

E-Learning content is ideally the sort of content that helps us work through the understanding and learning of formalized subject matter. E-Learning courseware is also lengthy, lasting from 30 minutes to over an hour in some cases. Learners have to be somewhere where they can focus.

It's not often very collaborative (although in recent times there's more and more collaboration built into E-Learning). Usually, E-Learning is a solitary, one-on-one learning interaction.

KEY POINT – E-Learning impacts career, certifications, and qualifications.

Of the three types of content I'm discussing in this session, I would suggest that E-Learning as training can best impact one's career. It underpins the learning one does for certifications and qualifications. E-Learning is extremely good when you have this type of requirement for formalized training. E-Learning finds its real niche when we're trying to teach or train a particular, formalized subject matter to a group of learners, and are supporting the learning activity using technology from a distance. Nowadays, learners can certify in a wide range of industry subject matter such as Insurance, Finance and Safety. With online testing, E-Learning courses have achieved acceptance as a professionally supported means of qualification.

KEY POINT – E-Learning addresses 'formal' corporate learning needs only.

We've seen a lot of surveys by the ASTD (now ATD) and other learning industry organizations that tell us E-Learning is only addressing twenty percent of our learning needs: the 'formal' needs.

The sorts of things that E-Learning does very well, such as certification training and career building, only address a part of the corporate training need. It's very good at addressing those, but E-Learning isn't good for mobile-based content for the reasons mentioned earlier. It isn't good for being pushed down the mobile channel without *modification*. Now, I'm not saying this can't be done. It can be, of course. I've seen a lot of content go down the mobile channel where it is being used to deliver E-learning. However, using mobile to do E-Learning is not ideal. And you should definitely not use E-Learning content for Social Learning or for social posting.

KEY POINT – E-Learning requires specific E-Learning technology and tools.

Another difference is that E-Learning requires specific E-Learning tools. These fall into two main types: 1) a Content Authoring Tool to develop the E-Learning content which is often published in SCORM format (see Standards later in this chapter), and 2) a Learning Management System (LMS), which is used to deliver the content, capture and track results, and manage the learner and instructor user-accounts. E-Learning requires a range of technologies which are well-established and mature, although they are also continually evolving.

The learning technology market has many offerings, so there's a wide range of tools to support E-Learning.

KEY POINT – E-Learning needs consultation and approvals.
E-Learning content development differs from Mobile and Social Learning content in that it typically demands consultation and approvals. You get together as a project group to discuss the requirements, and you do a needs analysis.

When creating E-Learning content, you storyboard out the idea and content. You try and capture everything in an all-encompassing piece of content. This is the ADDIE model mentioned before.

Consequently, there is a lot of consultation and approval required. It's time-consuming, and can involve a lot of people. This normally means that there's a high cost associated with it.

MOBILE LEARNING

Now, let's look at **Mobile Learning** because Mobile Learning is quite a bit different. Mobile Learning is typically about fast, rapid development. Mobile Learning should not really be E-Learning that's repurposed, or is simply delivered using mobile technology.

Definition:

Mobile Learning is training or knowledge delivered as digital content on a mobile device such as a tablet or smart phone. Mobile Learning content is a mix of formal and informal and is hosted in a variety of places, including (but not limited to) a Learning Management System.

KEY POINT – Mobile Learning uses rapid development.

Mobile Learning should ideally be rapidly developed. It can be less formalized than E-Learning in nature and as a consequence does not need to follow the same development process (ADDIE).

KEY POINT – Mobile Learning demands smart devices and access to mobile networks.

Mobile Learning also demands a smart device and very often one needs 3G or 4G on the mobile network.

Smart devices are shaping the way in which we think about Mobile Learning development and how Mobile Learning impacts competency. Three changes have already underlined this:

1. Smart device shipments recently outpaced personal computer shipments, meaning that they are now more widely-used than computers.

2. The **Bring Your Own Device (BYOD)** policy for managing employee mobile devices has emerged as a consequence of the proliferation of smart devices as a production tool. No organization can offer its employees the wide range of devices available in the market today, and no employee wants to carry two devices; one from the organization for work, and the other from a personal contract for personal use. So, organizations devised the BYOD policy which allows

employees to bring their own devices for use at work as a production tool.

3. Mobile application development has become more important than desktop software production (echoing point #1 above).

In many aspects, Mobile Learning is going to outpace other forms of learning activity in the years ahead.

KEY POINT – Mobile Learning can be managed at the Business Unit level.

Unlike E-Learning, Mobile Learning can be more often created and managed at the Business Unit level. The Business Units can work much more in this area taking the load away from the Training department as there is no need for Mobile Learning content to be developed exclusively by Training/L&D. A **Subject Matter Expert** (SME) in a Business Unit can easily pick an Authoring Tool and develop content for Mobile Learning. This allows the content to be developed faster and then rapidly uploaded for delivery to the learner. It doesn't need to go through the same formalized development process as E-Learning. It also means that content can be edited and updated by the person who knows most about the subject: The Subject Matter Expert.

KEY POINT – Mobile Learning addresses 'informal' corporate learning needs. It is used for On-the-Job-Training (OJT), Informal Learning and knowledge-sharing.

Another difference we have discovered is that Mobile Learning is very useful for 'informal' learning needs such as On-the-Job-Training (see chapter 6 with Marvin Mullins) where the learner needs immediate access to the content. Applications where pushing out content to a population of dispersed employees, such as sales engineers, sales people, insurance brokers, and those who need to get up-to-date, bite-sized bits of information on-the-go, are well suited to Mobile Learning. It's perfect for informal types of training and knowledge-sharing. Mobile Learning content is also great when used as part of a blended program such as 70:20:10 (see chapter 3 with Charles Jennings) where you are applying 'informal' activities for learning with formal E-learning.

Mobile Learning is very different from E-Learning in both content type and activity.

KEY POINT – Mobile Learning needs mobile servers, smart devices and rapid-development Authoring Tools.

Like E-learning, Mobile Learning also requires specific tools. You'll need mobile servers which manage the data across the mobile networks, deliver it to the learner, and pass the results to the Learning Management Server (LMS). You'll need an LMS if you want to do results tracking. You will require some easy-to-use and rapid Content Authoring Tools. Fortunately, there's a wide range of tools available that you can use for Mobile Learning, and in some cases, such as with an LMS, you may be able to use E-Learning products.

KEY POINT – Mobile Learning does not require standards compliance.

We don't really have many major standards applicable to Mobile Learning content. Obviously, we have to conform to file types that mobile supports such as SCORM .pdf, MP4 and MP3. Those standard types are supported, but they're supporting *file* types as opposed to other types of standards. If you wish to track learner results, you will need to ensure that your content complies with SCORM.

KEY POINT – Mobile Learning is a mixture of professional development and Business Unit development.

Mobile Learning still uses professional formal development, but it also makes use of informal development. Mobile Learning is regularly created by employees working outside the L&D department who use their mobile devices to create content and post. We're going to see a proliferation of tools start to enable this type of mobile content creation.

KEY POINT – Mobile Learning can deliver modified E-Learning content, but also delivers non-professionally-developed content. File size is an important consideration.

Mobile Learning can deliver E-Learning content with modification but it also facilitates non-professionally-developed content delivery. In Mobile Learning the use of video, images, audio and texts is commonplace. The type of content pushed out here is different because we concern ourselves more with keeping file sizes as small as possible to support fast transmission.

Restrictions on opportunities for employee interaction with the content are also a consideration. Interaction is not so easy to have when an employee is on a mobile device on a train or bus, for example. Theoretically, as long as they stay online an interaction can take place. But if they go offline, what do they do then? Can you create content that's interactive and download-able? Can it be interactive, suitable for mobile, and yet have results tracked and captured when the employee connects back online again? Simply re-purposing E-Learning for Mobile delivery will not work in many of these cases.

KEY POINT – Mobile Learning has a mix of high-cost and budget content.

In Mobile Learning we have a meeting ground as far as costs are concerned. We may have high production costs, but we can also have low-budget production costs. This is where we see professionally-produced content mixed with 'informal' employee-produced content. The latter is normally free of charge, as employees create content to share knowledge, and are not necessarily paid specifically to do so.

KEY POINT – Mobile Learning content is often 'bite-sized' learning.

Let's take a moment and think about the nature of Mobile Learning. There are often issues with bandwidth as the learner is mobile and passes through different network zones and signal areas. There are issues with file sizes because streaming large content often leads to interruptions in service due to drop-outs in signal. So E-Learning content, which is typically full of large-sized files, is not suitable for Mobile Learning without some modification. Mobile Learning is efficient when using small pieces of content pushed down to a widely-dispersed group of people for immediate consumption. This is one of the reasons why re-purposing E-Learning does not suit Mobile Learning. Sometimes, E-Learning is 'chunked' into smaller pieces for Mobile Learning consumption; but, again, this is very dependent on the content itself and is not appropriate without consideration of the application.

KEY POINT – Mobile Learning impacts competencies, skills, knowledge and actions.

What you know today, your 'competency', is your particular skill or area. It relates to how well you do your job. Performance support is something one can really drive well with Mobile Learning. It can be tailored so that it impacts one's particular knowledge. It can be personalized.

As an employee, mobile content and learning is going to help you to do your job better. It impacts competency. It impacts skill. It impacts knowledge. It impacts actions so that you learn something for immediate use as opposed to future use. When you're going to take knowledge and put it into practice now, use Mobile Learning. This is not something that's only theoretical. It has practical application in the workplace. Mobile content refers to something that one can apply now and today. So that's one difference that sets it apart from E-Learning that we need to think about when we're creating mobile content. E-Learning is good for formal training leading to certifications and compliance, whereas Mobile Learning is good for on-the-job practical use.

SOCIAL LEARNING

The third content type is Social Learning content. Let's now look at the characteristics of this.

Definition:
Social Learning is training or knowledge delivered as digital content. The learner interacts with other learners in social media and networks (communities) for the purpose of sharing, discussing and learning from each other. Social Learning content is hosted in a variety of areas, but rarely on a Learning Management System.

KEY POINT – Social Learning is about instantaneous development.
Social Learning has instantaneous development. It's at the speed of thought. It's content we're sending and sharing right now because we just saw it online and we think it's applicable, and there it goes. One click. We post it and it's gone. It's instantaneously developed. It's short. It's immediate. It's share-able.

KEY POINT – Social Learning is 'check-in and check-out'.

By 'check-in and check-out', I mean you 'drop into' the conversation. You post some content. You make a comment. You 'like' something you saw. You share a link, and then you get back to your other tasks. After a while, you drop back into the conversation or **'social feed'**, as it's called, and you update yourself. Technology-wise you're using social media, or enterprise social networks. It's this type of knowledge-sharing activity that you're supporting with Social Learning content.

KEY POINT – Social Learning is used for trust-building, connecting, linking, asking, sharing, etc.

Social Learning is used for trust-building and connecting to like-minded people. It's used for linking and it's used for asking and sharing. Social Learning content has to have interaction around it and a fast response time. It has to be content that's suitable for speed.

We learn about each other based upon what we post. We also learn about each other's competencies, and whether or not we want to follow others based on what they are saying in the conversation.

That equally applies to the content they have *referenced* on their posts. So it's this important aspect of content handling that we really see in Social Learning, and not in E-Learning or Mobile Learning.

KEY POINT – Social Learning demands social skills, social networks and participation.

Social Learning has some slightly different requirements: You have to be socially skilled. You should be thinking about contributing all the time. If everybody listened without participating, there wouldn't be much social interaction. You should be ready to commit to social interaction. You should be somebody who wants to participate. You should also be somebody who likes to use social networks and doesn't view them with suspicion or with some form of concern. Make sure you are part of the conversation and learn how to use social tools. This is a skill for the 21st Century. It's a competency we all need to have.

Now, not everybody understands how to work with social networks and how to use Social Learning. The type of learning activities we can support here are going to be different from that of E-Learning and, to a lesser degree, Mobile Learning. Social Learning requires a different mindset from the learner. It also demands a different mindset from the Learning and Development professional. It's a new competency we all have to acquire, but the benefits when we do have already been well-established by the organizations utilizing Social Learning successfully today.

KEY POINT – Social Learning is mainly non-professionally-developed, employee-made content.
Social Learning content is informally produced. It's normally employee-driven production. The main 'developers' are employees with a smart-device who create, post and share content for the benefit of their colleagues. This type of development is going to become highly present in corporate learning and knowledge-sharing. Social Learning has increased in popularity among learners and learning professionals and is gaining in usage. It is different from both E-Learning and Mobile Learning.

Social Learning content has a large *dependence* on employee development. This is not content that we submit to the training department for creation. It is immediate knowledge-sharing which, by its nature, means employees have to be the principle creators of content. It is composed of comments and link-sharing as well. Some organizations have internal video repositories (an internal YouTube). These have proven to be very successful as employees create their own videos to help their colleagues get work done.

KEY POINT – Social Learning content reinforces discussion points or context, has shared experience and is supported by links, video (YouTube), text messaging (Twitter), and other social media.

This is the type of thing that enables employees to do interactive posting. This is the value of social networks; even when you're isolated in the field, or doing your job, you're still connected to your mobile network.

Content reinforces social discussion of content. Social Learning content is very different when compared with E-Learning content; it involves capturing and sharing experiences, and then distributing it with social media.

Again, these are small bits of content that are helping us get our job done, but also helping us take part in the conversation. We're doing things as a group with Social Learning. It is collective learning.

KEY POINT – Social Learning is low-cost or free.

Social Learning is usually low-cost to do. Sometimes it's free if it's employee-created. Employees may recommend content that is seen in other places on the internet (for example on YouTube or websites), or create their own videos. Typically when we're posting or creating content as part of the discussion, we're doing it at a low cost or using free techniques.

KEY POINT – Social Learning addresses 'informal' corporate learning needs.

Social Learning addresses 'informal' learning needs because this is essentially the type of content we're posting (and sharing) to enable us to do our job. It involves all employees. This is about building up our competencies, enabling us to interact with each other and collaborate.

KEY POINT – Social Learning technologies are enterprise social networks, social media, media servers, and social data analysis tools.

Social Learning requires social networks. It requires easy publishing tools and media servers; so, again, we've got technology associated with Social Learning, but it's very different from E-Learning technology. This content doesn't often go on the LMS, but the content on the LMS can be shared via links posted in the social infrastructure. This content goes in social media and social networks. This presents a new challenge for analytics and business intelligence gathering tools. As you'd expect, we have the emergence of new tools to gather social data, slice-and-dice it, and serve it up in reports for business leaders to see what is going on in their social businesses. This is already starting to bleed into the Social Learning area, where there is great interest to understand what topics are trending with corporate learners.

KEY POINT – Social Learning demands employee empowerment and involvement, and Community management.

Employee empowerment and community management is something that is new and unique to Social Learning that we don't see in the other areas. Employee empowerment means everybody should be allowed to create content and should be able to take part in the conversation.

KEY POINT – Social Learning has no standards requirement.

There are no standards in Social Learning, but innovations like the **Experience API (XAPI)**, affectionately known as 'Tin Can' after the organization that is exploiting this standard from Adaptive Distributed Learning (ADL) Labs, will improve our understanding of learner behaviors. The 'Tin Can' API makes it possible to collect data about the learner's experience while doing a learning activity.

On a general social business theme, Social Learning can be supported by **social policies**. What do I mean by social policies? I mean policies that give guidelines on how the company wants to see its employees engaging using social discourse in social networks. So, not necessarily hard and fast rules saying "you cannot post this or that" (although that maybe the case in some sensitive areas), but instead say, "Think before you post. Think about what you're trying to achieve and post responsibly."

KEY POINT – Social Learning impacts thoughts, ideas, collaboration and knowledge exchange.

Social Learning is, in many ways, ideal for us to create content to post within programs such as 70:20:10, and other collaborative learning activities that we want our employees to take part in.

A FINAL WORD - RESPONSIVE DESIGN

Use of Responsive Design (Creation).

On the surface the three content types may look similar enough to lull developers into thinking they can develop once and publish to any platform. Certainly this would save time. However, there are some good reasons why that often won't work, and in this chapter I have raised legitimate concerns in context.

Responsive Design has a growing and popular role in *all* content development today. There has been a lot of recent discussion about **'Responsive Design'** being critical to development.

What is Responsive Design?

Responsive Design ensures that the presentation of the page looks the same regardless of the device it is being displayed on.

Now, if you follow a "develop-once-publish-to-multiple-platform" strategy, it is true that Responsive Design will save time and deliver a uniform content page. However, we have seen why that strategy is not necessarily an effective approach for these three types of learning content.

CHAPTER ONE KEY POINT SUMMARY

WHAT A DIFFERENCE GOOD CONTENT MAKES

E-LEARNING

DEFINITION

E-Learning is training delivered as digital content, which learners work through from computers, often at a distance, in their own offices or homes. E-Learning consists of formal content and is hosted on a Learning Management System, which the learner accesses via a browser, and which tracks and stores the learner's results.

E-Learning is developed and produced by the Training or Learning and Development (L&D) department.

E-Learning addresses formal corporate learning needs.

E-Learning requires specific E-Learning technology and tools.

E-Learning needs consultation and approvals.

E-Learning follows standards.

E-Learning takes time to develop and complete.

E-Learning is used for formal training and compliance.

E-Learning demands learner focus, a quiet place and user interaction.

E-Learning impacts career, certifications, and qualifications.

E-Learning uses high quality development and production.

E-Learning has high use of professional video, graphic design, animations, interactivity, storyboards, Gamification and testing.

E-Learning has high production costs, in-house and outsourced content development, and bought-in content is common.

MOBILE LEARNING

DEFINITION

Mobile Learning is training or knowledge delivered as digital content on a mobile device such as a tablet or smart phone. Mobile Learning content is a mix of formal and informal and is hosted in a variety of places, including (but not limited to) a Learning Management System.

Mobile Learning is a mixture of professional development and Business Unit development.

Mobile Learning requires smart devices and access to mobile networks.

Mobile Learning addresses informal corporate learning needs such as On-the-Job-Training (OJT), Informal learning and knowledge-sharing.

Mobile Learning needs mobile servers, smart devices and rapid Content Authoring Tools.

Mobile Learning can be managed at Business Unit level.

Mobile Learning does not require standards compliance.

Mobile Learning uses rapid development.

Mobile Learning uses 'bite-sized' learning.

Mobile Learning impacts competencies, skills, knowledge, and actions.

Mobile Learning can deliver modified E-Learning content but also delivers non-professionally developed content; uses standard file types such as MP4, .pdfs, MP3, etc.

Mobile Learning has a mix of high cost and budget content.

SOCIAL LEARNING

DEFINITION

Social Learning is training or knowledge delivered as digital content. The learner interacts with other learners in social media and networks (communities) for the purpose of sharing, discussing and learning from each other. Social Learning content is hosted in a variety of areas, but rarely on a Learning Management System.

Social Learning has mainly non-professionally-developed, employee-made content.

Social Learning addresses informal corporate learning needs.

Social Learning technologies are Enterprise Social Networks, social media, media servers, and social data analysis tools.

Social Learning demands employee empowerment and involvement, and Community management.

Social Learning has no standards requirement.

Social Learning has instantaneous development.

Social Learning is 'check-in and check-out'.

Social Learning is used for trust-building, connecting, linking, asking, and sharing.

Social Learning demands social skills, uses social networks, and participation.

Social Learning content reinforces discussion points or context, is a shared experience, and is supported by links, video (YouTube), text messaging (Twitter), and other social media.

Social Learning is low-cost or free.

CHAPTER 3

TECHNOLOGY ENHANCED

LEARNING

IN

70:20:10

WITH

CHARLES JENNINGS

70:20:10 - A Framework for High Performance Development Practices.

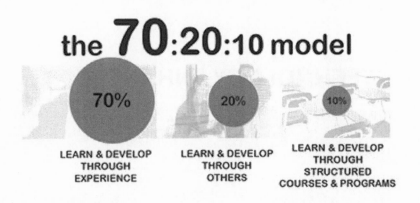

Over the past few years the 70:20:10 model for development has captured the imagination of organizations across the world.

Some organizations apply 70:20:10 principles to targeted and specific development solutions. Others use it more strategically as a way to help them rethink and re-position their wider learning philosophies.

The 70:20:10 framework is a simple concept that has developed from work carried out by various researchers over the past half-century that suggests a one-dimensional focus on structured training and development – a rut that many organizations had fallen into – misses the opportunity to exploit learning and development where most of it happens, which is within the work-flow.

A Reference Model, not a Recipe

It's important to be aware that 70:20:10 is a reference model and not a recipe. The numbers are not a rigid formula. They simply remind us of the facts above – that the majority of learning and development comes through experiential and social learning in the workplace (the '70' and '20') rather than through formal classes and courses (the '10'). Of course structured and directed 'formal' learning can help, but it rarely, if ever, provides the complete answer.

If you acknowledge that high performers usually build their capabilities through experience, through practice and through utilizing a rich network of support rather than exclusively (or even mainly) through structured training and development away from the workplace, then you will immediately grasp the 70:20:10 concept.

Why Have So Many Organizations Adopted 70:20:10?

One answer to this question lies in the fact that 70:20:10 offers an easily-understood scaffolding that can be readily adapted to re-focus development across a much wider canvas than that traditionally used by HR and Learning professionals.

Why is this important?

It's important because research over the past 40 years at least has indicated that learning that occurs outside of formal classes and courses is not only more frequent but also generally more effective than its structured and 'managed' counterpart.

It's also important because the 70:20:10 framework provides a way to integrate currently disparate development activities – such as leadership programs, informal coaching and mentoring, and the extraction of learning from work through conversations, communities, sharing, reflective practice and other actions. It also provides a coherent framework to strategize workplace, social and structured learning activities.

Although the 70:20:10 framework applies to all adult learning, it is particularly relevant when thinking about building a strategy to develop and support high performers.

Most organizations aspire to further develop their high performers, and to develop others to become high performers, as it is the high performing cadre that drives successful organizations.

Research by the Corporate Executive Board suggests that 'enterprise contributors' (as it calls the small cadre of high performers) can increase organizational revenue and profits by as much as 12%. That often means the difference between success and failure.

A Profile of High Performers

If we look at a generic profile of a high performer through a 70:20:10 'lens' the following is clear:

1. High performers have usually quickly mastered the basics. This was achieved often, but not always, using structured development approaches.

This is where the '**10**' of formal learning and development through courses and programs can help people new to an organization or role get 'up-to-speed' quickly and efficiently.

2. They have spent hundreds of hours using practice, trial-and-error, and self-testing to hone their capabilities.

   Some of this experiential learning and reflective practice may be structured (the '**10**'). Alternatively it may be part of the work-flow (the '**70**' and '**20**')

3. They are embedded in their professional community both within and outside their organization. They regularly share their expertise across their network and also call on colleagues as informal coaches and mentors when they need advice and help.

   This vital part of any high performer's arsenal sits firmly in the '**20**' part of the framework.

4. They have on-the-job performance support at fingertips. They

know where to find the answers to the challenge-at-hand, whether it is via their own PKM (personal knowledge management) resources or simply by knowing who will be best able to help them.

Performance support comes in many forms. It may be embedded in workflow tools (where most of the ePSS tools and systems provide support), or be accessed through 'others' across the high performer's network. As such, this element can sit in both the '**20'** and '**70'** parts of the framework.

5. They have undertaken thousands of hours of experience and reflection, sometimes alone, sometimes with their manager and team, and sometimes with their professional network.

These activities are critical for high performance. They all sit within the '**70'** and '**20'** domains of the framework.[1]

---

1 Reproduced from his 70:20:10 Blog with kind permission of Charles Jennings. For more information about 70:20:10 you may be interested to buy Charles's new book "70:20:10 and Beyond" available from August 2015.

Simon Birt: Good morning, everyone, and welcome. Today, we're going to be talking with Charles Jennings, who is a proponent, a long time consultant, and expert in the area of 70:20:10. We're going to be discussing some aspects regarding the framework and how we support 70:20:10 with technology today.

70:20:10: A learning framework employed by many organizations which addresses and exploits Workplace and Social Learning to generate higher performance outcomes from employees.

Charles Jennings has helped many organizations build and implement 70:20:10 strategies. He's been working with 70:20:10 approaches for 15 years and implemented 70:20:10 when he was the Chief Learning Officer in a FTSE 100 global company (Reuters). I'll leave it to him to explain what he did and how that was implemented. Hello, Charles.

Charles Jennings: Hello, Simon.

Simon Birt: *Welcome to the session. First of all, could you describe what you do today to help organizations develop 70:20:10 strategies and apply them?*

Charles Jennings: Well, I think organizations have found the 70:20:10 framework very helpful, more as a change agent than anything else, in that it really extends learning. So, it helps us look at learning across the board. I've worked with more than a hundred organizations, and there are generally two approaches that we find we're taking.

One is what I call the **evolutionary** approach, which is building on blended learning. It's how can we make more use of what is already blended to think about how we exploit Social Learning, how we exploit Experiential Learning, how we take that out into the work-flow. It might include incorporating E-Learning into the work-flow, or linking classroom learning into the workplace. So that's One. As said, that's an evolutionary step from what's been done in the past to sort of stretch that out.

evolutionary

- Build on 'blending' learning

- Incorporate eLearning into the workflow

- Link classroom learning into the workplace

revolutionary

- Help 'enrol' senior leadership

- Assist transformation mindset

- Develop 70:20:10 strategy

- Help build new skills and capabilities

The other area, which is where I spend most of my time working with organizations, is what I call the **revolutionary** approach, which is where we're looking at making some significant changes. And it's very much around a transformation mindset, developing a new strategy in order to help organizations develop high performance. I do a lot of work around helping what I call 'enrolling senior leadership'. In other words, talking to groups of senior leaders to get them to understand the potential benefits, and why these sorts of developments are really important.

And I also work in helping to build new skills and capabilities, because once you get into 70:20:10, you enhance the traditional skill sets of many learning and training professionals in designing, developing, and delivering content. You need to build on those. There's a whole new range of skills that are required. So these are some of the areas that I tend to work in.

Simon Birt: *Do you find that either one of these works better than another? What is it that helps you decide which one is the right one to apply?*

Charles Jennings: Well, it's all about context, actually. It's like everything in life. Certainly, I always recommend that organizations look at potential, and carry out proof of concept and pilots because that's the best way to put this into practice. For example, perhaps you're simply taking a classroom program that you've got, and you're thinking of how you can add learning into that. That's one thing. That's a technical approach, I guess. But, as another example,

I've been working with the Philips Company in the Netherlands where they're going through a large transformation and transforming all of their development based around 70:20:10. The situation in Philips is about readiness for what I call a 'revolutionary change'. In other words, a whole transformation. So it really depends on the context, and the real value comes out of the right-hand side, out of the revolutionary change, although there's a lot of value that can come out of any individual development. That's for sure.

Simon Birt: *And do you find that when a company arrives at the decision to take the revolutionary approach, they've come there because of a failure in the existing learning programs they're using, or is there something else that's bringing them to that kind of overall overhaul of what they currently do?*

Charles Jennings: It comes from various points. Sometimes, it's simply that the senior executive or a senior person in the organization has maybe read something, or been to a conference and heard someone mention 70:20:10, and asked, "What's this all about?", and then thought, "Well, this fits for us." Or, it can be that, in some organizations, there are increasing pressures and they feel that they need to get the best value they possibly can out of their people.

That means that individuals, teams, and the organization need to perform at the highest possible level. They're looking for ways in which they can change that. In some cases, they're finding that what they've been doing in the past has not worked and they really need to make the changes. At other times, it's simply how to improve on what they've got.

Simon Birt: *Okay. So let's move on to the next question: How do you relate the 70:20:10 thinking to today's workplace challenges? Are there some key principles that you apply?*

Charles Jennings: Well, I think there are, but they're not a simple, succinct set of principles. You can see in the illustration that these are the major challenges that most organizations are facing, and we know all of these. There are issues of impact; how can we make sure that the work that's done in terms of Learning and Development training has impact, and how do we reduce time to performance? Certainly, when I went into Reuters I found that there were some on-boarding programs that lasted three months for roles where people only stayed in those roles for twenty-one months. So that clearly was not appropriate, not the best way to work. You needed to look at that and do something about it.

There are issues around sustainability. For example, have we got solutions that are sustainable and scale-able? And one of the major, major challenges that we've had with the classroom model, (and I'm not saying the classroom doesn't work at all. I think classroom is highly appropriate if you're trying to develop particular attitudes and values and so on; it's really very valuable to get people together), but if you're simply transferring information and building knowledge, classroom is probably the most inefficient, ineffective way to do it. It's not sustainable, and it's resource-hungry, and all those sorts of things. So there are those issues.

There are issues around innovation. Are we innovating across our organization in an appropriate way? And that means innovating in the way which would develop capability and Learning and Development.

the challenges

impact
time to performance
sustainability
innovation
cost constraint

Organizations need on average 27% higher employee performance to reach their goals. However, work is more complex, interconnected, and dynamic than ever before.

"Succeeding in this environment is not about doing more things, it's about doing things differently".

Corporate Executive Board
October 2014

And lastly, there's the whole issue of cost constraint. Most organizations have to assess cost. They're continually looking at how they can save money, and how they can improve efficiency. I've got a quote here from the Corporate Executive Board that was just published last month, and I do quite a lot of work with the Corporate Executive Board. They surveyed 7,000 senior managers asking them, "What sort of increase in employee performance do they need in order to reach their goals over the next 12 months?" And the answer came back 27%, which is really a huge uplift. And then, in fact, the Corporate Executive Board looked at how, using traditional methods, that would play out. And they came to the view that, using classic classroom methods, only 4% could be added because we're better at doing classroom training and it works pretty well so there's not a lot of benefits we can sweat out. So they came to the view that we need to do something else.

we now know that:

- people learn more about their work informally than formally
- novices will learn a greater proportion formally than veterans
- veterans will rely more on informal learning
- formal learning works best with explicit
- Informal learning works best with **tacit**

It's not about doing more, it's about doing things differently. And actually, those are the key challenges. I also think that the principle that I use for 70:20:10 is that we know a few things about the way adults learn.

Jay Cross, who I do quite a lot of work with, has written a very good book around 'Informal Learning', which was the genesis of this because we know that people learn more about their work informally than formally. We know that they learn more about the work in the workplace than they do when they're away from work. Novices, those people who are new to a role, or new to an organization, will rely more on formal structure than a veteran, someone who has been in a role or in an organization for a long time. In fact, I often ask senior leaders, "How many courses or programs have you been on in the last year?" And the response I usually get is a laugh because, if you've been in an organization for quite a while, it's unlikely that formal training is going to help you move the bar.

We also know, and these last two points are critical, that formal structured development works really well when we have explicit information; when the information is all described, it's clear, it's not changing, and we know that there are certain situations where it will be applied. But, when we're dealing with tacit information, we know that learning through Social Learning, or through Experiential Learning, through knowing the right person to ask, the right question and so on, is much, much more effective. And, in fact, all the research, - McKenzie did some work on this in the U.S.A – has shown that when you look at the number of jobs that are being created, many more jobs are created that need people to deal with tacit information; jobs that require decision-making and dealing with ambiguity and so on, whereas the amount of transactional work is sort of flat-lining. The ability to deal with tacit information and turn that into tacit knowledge and into action is becoming increasingly important. They're the principles for thinking about how do you move Learning and Development out beyond the structure, utilize the structure for where it works well, and then get out into the 20 and the 70 pieces.

Simon Birt: *There's a quotation from the Corporate Executive Board about how work is becoming more complex and integrated with more touch points throughout an organization than it might have had some time ago. And, I suspect that there's technology behind the drive of some of this. But are you also thinking that we're changing the way we work? Not just driven by technology, but in other ways that impact the way that we should be thinking about learning?*

Charles Jennings: Absolutely, especially around complexity. I hardly know any organization that doesn't have, or hasn't had a program which is based around simplicity or simplification, because most organizations realize that work is becoming more complex. We all try to simplify things and sometimes that works; sometimes it doesn't. But, be that as it may, most of us are working in more complex environments than we were 10 years ago. And I would just ask people who are listening to this conversation: Is your work, your working environment, and what you have to do now more complex than it was 10 or 15 years ago? Almost invariably, it is. Yet a lot of our training models were based around pretty straightforward, transactional, industrial processes. We were training people to do repetitive work, work where we could predict the sorts of problems that we were going to face. Nowadays, most of us who earn our living with our heads rather than our hands will know that the problems that we come up against everyday are unique, or that we're unlikely to see very often if they're not unique. And so how do you prepare people for dealing with those problems? The answer is that you have to think more about developing people's learning skills, rather than developing their knowledge of content and process because that content and process will change. So I think that again is another sort of driver around these changes.

Simon Birt: *Well, to that point, several surveys of CEOs by such bodies as the Harvard Business Review have highlighted in recent articles and research that creativity and problem-solving are actually more important in many ways than what you know, especially now that knowledge is at our fingertips. With the internet, you can find out something very quickly. But it's very hard to train somebody to know* *how to problem-solve, or how to be creative at work. I suspect that, to remain competitive, companies are thinking about how they train their staff to do these types of activities rather than - as you've said - repetitive work.*

Charles Jennings: Yes, those core skills are critical. One of those core skills is meta-learning, in other words becoming efficient learners rather than anything else because situations will change and information will change. Everything will change, so we've got to be capable more than ever of working in that changing world more effectively.

Simon Birt: *You found that 70:20:10 is a good way to do this. Can you share with us the types of activities you would typically expect a 70:20:10 organization to be engaged in as opposed to one that isn't practicing this type of framework?*

Charles Jennings: Yes, certainly. In the following image I have put just a small subset of the sorts of activities that I often work with organizations on and talk about in 70:20:10. We could argue some of these: the 70 being learning through experience and practice; the 20 being learning through conversations, networks, working with others; and the 10 being learning in a structured way. Of course, it's not set in stone. You can't say that something always fits in the 70 or the 20 or the 10 bucket. In fact, the buckets overlap. This is one of the key messages I try to get across to people: 70:20:10 is not, first of all, about the numbers. It's about change. The numbers help us think, and remind us that a lot of learning occurs through social and experiential learning, and how we support that. In this image are some of the sorts of activities that you'd expect an organization utilizing the 70:20:10 model would be using. They'd have ways in which they could, for example, support learning in real situations. How do we help people solve problems as part of the work flow?

How are we using reflection? Not just individual reflection, but also reflective practice through teams. We're building an organizational knowledge pool basically by sharing what goes well, what doesn't, and reflecting and sharing about this. Then there are all sorts of things such as mentoring and reverse mentoring, informal coaching and effective feedback to consider.

70) Encouraging learning through daily work and assignments

70) Supporting learning in real situations

70) Using problems solving as a learning technique

70) Using special assignments for development

70) Individual reflection

70) Job swaps and shadowing for development

70) Community activities as a development activity

70) Using team project de-briefs as a learning tool

20) Mentoring and reverse mentoring

20) Coaching and encouraging informal feedback

20) Building and ex[external networl

20) Using team meetings for reflection and learning

20) Exploiting professional associations as a development resource

20) Using action learning

10) Providing structured classroom programmes

10) Providing activity-based workshops

10) Offering seminars and masterclasses

10) Using eLearning

10) E-Labs or other virtual learning environments

We're looking at all of these sorts of things and thinking about how we can support them as learning and training professionals. When we start to look at the 70 and 20, we can't control them but we can support them. We can facilitate them and we can help them happen. We can learn from them. And I think that's one of the key changes that learning and training professionals need to understand. That these things are really important, but they're not things that you can pack up and put in a nice box and deliver. There are things that we think about. Do we have the infrastructures to support them? Do we have an infrastructure meaning technical infrastructure and people? And do we have the processes that we can provide to our organization to facilitate them? Some of them are straightforward such as Action Learning. Action Learning is a pretty well-defined process of collaborative problem-solving, and there are various approaches to it. There is a good model there. We are using this because it is a great method. I've seen some organizations where they've taken their structured learning, removed some of the residential components, and put these into Action Learning sets. It's worked really well extending learning into the work place.

Simon Birt: *You've talked about a combination of four activities in the past and they are: Experience, Practice, Conversation and Reflection. Let's elaborate on that in the context of what we have just been talking about. I'm intrigued by this idea of creating spaces for reflection. I know that this happens in tech companies like Google and so on. They have lots of play-spaces to encourage creativity and thinking, but does this really apply to an insurance company, for example? Is it practical? Is it something that can be done?*

Charles Jennings: Yes. Let me work backwards then. That reflection piece is really critical. I've had so many conversations with people working in high pressure jobs where they say, "This is all very well and good but we don't really have time for reflection," and my answer to that is always, "You don't have time not to reflect."

I'll often tell a story about Rafa Nadal, the tennis player, who is a compulsive reflector. He's actually learned how to reflect, and he has a few seconds to reflect after each play on what happened, what went well, what didn't go well, what he would do differently, and then he has to get on with it. I've seen some organizations use reflective practice really, really well. It's absolutely critical.

new and challenging **experiences**

opportunities for **practice**

rich **conversations and networks**

spaces for **reflection**

I often say, if you boil down the way adults learn in the workplace, where we walk out of the door at home and we walk into our workplace, how are we going to learn? We learn principally through these four different approaches, through facing new and challenging experiences, and then reflecting on them and learning through things going well or not going well.

We learn through the opportunity to practice. An example is someone like Federer that's on the top right image here. If we think that Roger Federer remains at the top of his game simply by playing competitions, we're crazy. Of course he's back on the court practicing all the time, and we understand that top sportsmen and women practice all the time, yet we think within our own professional work, we don't need to practice. But we do. And thirdly, rich conversations and networks are absolutely critical. In fact, Rob Cross, who's the leading person in the world around social network analysis, wrote a great paper with IBM a few years ago, called "It's not what you know but who you know that gets work done in organizations." Having those networks and being able to have those conversations is critical. And then reflection. So those four for me are really important, and I always say to people, "Hold up your E-Learning course, or your classroom course. Hold these four up against those courses and see if they are augmenting and helping people have rich, new experiences, practice conversations and reflection, and – if they're not - go back and redesign it. Because, if they're simply transferring information, you might as well put it on parchment. You could probably do it cheaper, or do it some other sort of way. Yes, I think those four elements are absolutely critical in terms of 70:20:10.

Simon Birt: *We have talked on the sessions that I've hosted before about how we map technology that's emerging into new learning activities. How does technology support and deliver the 70:20:10 framework, things like social networks, our ability to deploy mobile and other technologies, really help us to support what you're talking about in those four areas?*

Charles Jennings: I think technology is really critical. We don't need technology all the time and, in fact, my colleague Jay Cross has said that conversation is the greatest learning technology ever invented. To a certain extent, I agree with that. But I think we do need technology because of the way we work, because of increasing complexity, because of the fact that many of us work in organizations that are spread across time and distance. Technology such as social technologies, or the social media, whether being used for social support, or actually being used for professional communities, or expert location, or whatever it happens to be is important. So, as well as the social technologies, there's all the performance support technologies. For me, that's already critical. How often are we in the middle of doing our work, and we find we need to know how to do something urgently? How can I best do this now? And those organizations that have grasped this, and understand that actually there are ways that we can use technology to link together the problem and the answer through some sort of performance support tool are making headway into this challenge.

With Mobile, obviously, the developments that are going around mobile technologies are really critical because many of us don't work from one time and from one location. Mobile technologies are important. I've seen some really good examples of using technologies over the last two or three years with user generated content, particularly around video. Organizations are using what I call 'internal YouTube', where experts are talking about what they do or demonstrating what they do. In fact, at British Telecom 10 years ago, the Chief Learning Officer of British Telecom surveyed the engineers at British Telecom and asked them, "If a new process or product was being released, how would you like to learn about it?"

And 72% of them said, "I'd like to learn from another engineer." Following that, BT put in a social-video, social-support system.

Simon Birt: *That's something that companies can definitely support and put in place relatively easily using today's technologies. You've obviously worked in 70:20:10 for a long time. Tell us a little bit about some of the benefits that you've seen organizations reach from here.*

Charles Jennings: When you boil it down, there are two key areas where benefits are generated: one is in efficiency and the other is in increased effectiveness. Efficiency means that we're able to do more with less; we're able to utilize the right approach for the right solution. When I was a Chief Learning Officer at Reuters and then Thompson Reuters, we always recommended to people approaching 70:20:10 to submit their review costs. Certainly at Reuters, we were able to generate really significant efficiency by utilizing 70:20:10 approaches and looking at how we developed people. One example comes from when we had a major technical training issue for some of our 5,000 technologists. Rather than putting them through structured programs and courses, we actually got them together in groups, provided them with pizzas, and let them talk. We let people who were working with different projects talk about their challenges and share them with each other. Subsequent to that, I have often said the best money I ever spent of my budget at Reuters was on pizzas because it was very successful.

So there is efficiency. But then the other bit, which I think is probably even more critical, is the effectiveness. And it goes back to the point about I made about novices and veterans, and the way that we learn in terms of informal and formal, and dealing with tacit and explicit knowledge. Effectiveness, in terms of what this does, is to open up a whole new avenue of different solutions that we can bring to bear to help solve our performance problems. By extending learning into the work-flow, we've got lots more opportunities for development. We can use the ones which are going to have the greatest effectiveness, and solve our problems more quickly, more effectively, more sustainably, rather than what we had up until 20 years ago, a one shot solution which was to bring people in the classroom. That evolved into a double-barrel solution, where we bring them into a classroom, and we give them E-Learning.

Now we've got a whole range of different solutions, some of which are driven by training and development, some of which are supported by training and development, but also possibly driven by team leaders and managers, or other areas of the organization. Organizations have found real benefits out of this when you look at the organizations that are using 70:20:10: companies like Amex, like Lego, like Bank of America, like Shell; I mean, I can go on and on and on. They're not using it because they just think it's a cute thing to do. They're using it because it's bringing some real benefit to them, whether benefits of efficiency or benefits of effectiveness, and most probably the benefits of both.

Simon Birt: *Yes. What would be the key considerations for implementing a 70:20:10 framework for people who have been listening today, do you think?*

Charles Jennings: I think that there are probably four considerations. Mindset is the major one because 70:20:10 is a change process. You have all sorts of change management issues, but mindset is really critical. That is moving from a mindset about where learning is something that occurs in one time, in one place, to thinking about learning in context and learning as a continuous process. That mindset change is required for senior leaders, line managers, line leaders, HR and also for Learning and Training people.

1) mindset
2) importance of context in learning
3) fit with organizational vision and aspirations
4) tools and approaches

There's also the need to think about context. I think that's a real consideration because we've known for years and years that people learn better in context. In fact, Bersin by Deloitte did a study two years ago now where they showed that people in organizations that use social media well for talent development are about three times better at development than others. And there's all sorts of research that supports that.

Aligning with your organizational vision and aspirations is essential. If you try to make a change that's at odds with how your organization works - unless you have senior leadership support to make those changes - you'll find you'll hit your head against a brick wall. So it's important to work on that.

And, lastly and certainly far from least, having the right tools and approaches. Having tools that can support learning in context and can support work which is actually done away from the classroom.

We should think about learning in terms of whether we're extending learning out of the workplace by adding learning into work; whether we're embedding learning in work through performance support or social support; or whether we're sharing and extracting learning from work. These are additional considerations to think about.

Simon Birt: *And finally, if a company already has some E-Learning or distance E-Learning programs, what would you say are the immediate steps they could take to just start?*

Charles Jennings: If you're already doing E-Learning, you can think about how to extend it out. For example, if we've got some programs already, how can we extend those out by adding them into the work-flow? Do we think about how we could replace some of the things we're doing in terms of our programs, or could we redefine them? Again, I've seen this done where a program has been sliced up into little micro-pieces of learning, so that people can actually extract what they need when they need it at a point of need. And, are we using social tools? Are we using approaches in which people can extract their learning while they work?

There's a whole movement around narrating or what they call "working out loud". How do we narrate our work? How we talk about our work? How do we share that with our communities? How do we work within our communities? So I think the world is our oyster in terms of how we approach these questions.

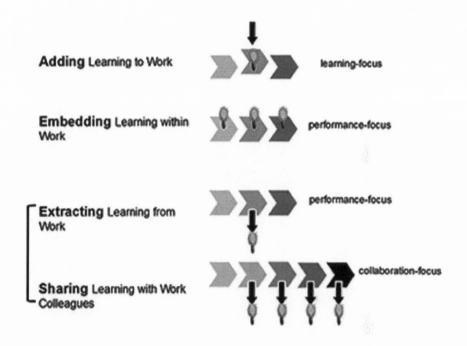

Simon Birt: *Thank you, Charles. For more information about 70:20:10, buy Charles's groundbreaking book entitled "70:20:10," or visit him at his blog: charles-jennings.blogspot.com.*

Charles Jennings: Thank you very much, Simon.

SIMON BIRT

CHAPTER 4

E-LEARNING

IN

THE CLOUD

WITH

SIMON BIRT

Cloud Computing - as we know - is on the rise, but is this just hype? Are we actually using Cloud services more in our companies and in our organizations or are we using it less, and how does it apply to your learning?

How effective is the use of Cloud in E-Learning and how can learning and development best benefit from using Cloud services and working with Cloud?

We've had a lot of discussion about Cloud; but, I'm not convinced that we're all using Cloud as effectively or as much as we could be, and the forecast for future use is definitely good. There is going to be more use of Cloud for learning, but we're also going to see a change in the way that we're deploying and using it.

First of all, I have a definition about Cloud to set the context for the chapter. Amazon.com is one of the largest Cloud Service Providers in the world at the moment and they define Cloud Computing as follows:

Definition:

The term "Cloud Computing" refers to the On-Demand delivery of IT resources via the internet with pay-as-you-go pricing.

If you're taking services from the Cloud but you're not paying through pay-as-you-go pricing then you're not really using *Cloud-as-a-service*. That is the first point. You're using the Cloud as a deployment but you're not using it as a service because theoretically you should be able to turn it off and turn it on according to your needs. That's really an essential point about the Cloud business model.

BENEFITS OF THE CLOUD BUSINESS MODEL

What are the main benefits of the Cloud business model? For people who aren't that familiar with what Cloud is about, let's examine why we use Cloud today. The reasons behind this relates to the benefits Cloud Computing brings us.

The concept of delivering IT resources as a service is not new. The delivery of centralized IT resources has been around for decades, since the development of the first large computers in the 1950s. In fact, the initial cost of computing was so high that sharing computing power was the only way to make it accessible.

What is new is the opportunity the internet brings to deliver these services as a utility to businesses and consumers, much like electricity or water. This is where the pay-as-you-go business model was borrowed from. The utility industry is the model for the Cloud-Computing financial model. Before the internet, centralized IT was the specialist domain of organizational IT. It was the main-frame computing model where one large computer called a 'main-frame' had hundreds of terminals plugged into it, where employees did data entry, and accessed the information held on it. The main-frame was the computer and the terminals were the access device, or interface.

When the internet became mainstream in the 1990s, the potential arose for centralizing and pooling computer resources that everyone with a device could access. Initially this was referred to as 'grid computing' - you may have heard of that term as well - which really does describe the idea of utility IT resources; it even borrowed the term 'grid' from the electricity industry. But it's essentially all about delivering services from a large computer, a mainframe, or a server to your desktop, laptop, or to your smart device via the browser; in other words *via the internet,* as the Amazon.com definition says.

However, it took a financial crisis and companies coming under pressure to cut costs that really launched the Cloud Computing business model as a mainstream viable alternative to having in-house IT resources. In 2000 and 2001 the 'dot.com' crisis started this movement, and in 2007 the Sub-Prime Mortgage crisis drove the impetus harder. In a drive to economize, companies began to cut their IT budgets and staff, and the Cloud Computing service providers started to provide centralized services at a pay-as-you-go price that was much lower than it had been versus in-house IT. Many non-critical or non-sensitive applications started to go to Cloud Computing. In the last ten years this business model has evolved, becoming stronger, more secure, and inevitably more attractive. In the next few years it will increase usage and probably grow to dominate IT resource delivery as we move more and more to the Mobile internet and smart device computing.

Cloud Computing, then, is here to stay for the foreseeable future. And there are substantial benefits to be gained in the Learning industry as much as any other. So what are the benefits?

KEY POINT – Low, ongoing cost

One of the key reasons that Cloud Computing is growing so rapidly is because it saves us money. There's a low ongoing cost and flexible payment plans to suit all budgets, without any loss in quality of IT services.

KEY POINT – No infrastructure investment expenses

The second thing that's attractive about Cloud is that generally speaking there are no upfront or ongoing infrastructure expenses because the Cloud Service Provider takes those on. So, for example, if you use Microsoft within your company, you have probably noticed in the last few years that it has developed a service called Office 365 or Microsoft 365. This is where Microsoft has put Office and other applications that you have used on your desktop into the Cloud, and now you can use those services in the Cloud for a monthly fee.

Now, the big benefit for companies is that - first of all - they pay for that as a service, so they're paying with low ongoing cost. The second thing to note is that you no longer have to invest in large infrastructure upgrades to run those services for your organizations because Microsoft is investing in the IT and the hardware to deliver that service to you. So there are no infrastructure expenses.

KEY POINT – Focus resources away from IT to core business

The third thing that's really important is that it allows you to focus resources *not* on managing IT or IT infrastructure, but on your business. So this again speaks to the issues we had during the financial crisis after the dot.com bubble burst.

As stated above, the two most recent major financial crises highlighted having to cut staff to survive. The jobs that companies had before no longer existed, and one of the areas that was heavily hit was IT. And the question arose: how to continue to manage IT at the same levels of quality of service with less staff? The answer is that companies started managing IT by going into Cloud and now the Cloud Service Provider takes on that responsibility. We have outsourced our IT, if you like. But now companies can take their human resources and focus them on business instead. It's a win-win business model. Companies now hire staff to go into areas of business which are considered 'core' (central to the business).

KEY POINT – Flexible usage plans

The fourth benefit that I have to mention is Flexible Usage Plans. The implication here for us in the Learning and Development business is that now we can pay for our applications on a project-by-project basis, which is very efficient. We can try tools without committing to them until we know they are useful and easy to use.

So, if these tools are provided to us through the Cloud then we can pay for them in the same way that we would pay for other IT services in the Cloud.

KEY POINT – Faster time to market and global reach

This final benefit I want to cover is sometimes a very underestimated point, but important for larger companies or for companies developing an international or a global strategy with a large number of employees.

Expansion of business is always dependent on logistics. Building out an IT infrastructure was a big factor in any planning. It still is today, but with Cloud Computing it needn't hold you back. If IT services are in the Cloud, a company can expand much more quickly and still deliver high quality computing services to staff. Furthermore, this implies that global reach is also closer.

Faster times to market and global reach means being able to very quickly deliver service and deliver work across the globe without having to make these investments in IT and human services. This is very important for companies that are trying to expand, or trying to manage global growth.

As we develop, we know that we're becoming more and more global. The world is getting smaller and so we've got to be able to deliver our business models within the global context. This is an ideal way to do that. Cloud *enables* us as far as IT is concerned. It enables us to deliver technology with a faster time to market and a more global reach.

So Cloud has a lot of benefits. But how does it apply to Learning today?

E-LEARNING AND SOFTWARE-AS-A-SERVICE

Let's look at how I've broken E-Learning down into various areas as far as technology is concerned.

KEY POINT - Content creation based in the Cloud

One of the things I'm going to look at is content creation and authoring, which is something that we normally do on the desktop.

Not many companies that I've dealt with have actually got a comprehensive model for working online for content creation, but that's just a matter of time. Cloud applies to E-Learning in the sense that we're going to see a change in content creation and authoring as it moves to the Cloud. This is something that's going to happen in the next few years.

KEY POINT – Management and Tracking

Management and tracking of content and learner results is something we're familiar with. Most LMS services these days can be acquired or can be paid for as a Cloud service. We may not choose to do that for reasons of security of content and confidentiality, but - in effect - we can use the Cloud for our management and our tracking. We can have an LMS or a content management server in the Cloud without any difficulty; those solutions exist.

KEY POINT – Browsers and Mobile Applications

Consider the move to mobile app distribution as well. This is an important one that's just starting to really come to the fore and give us some emphasis behind delivery of learning content. The developments in smart devices and the change in usage to smart devices from PCs and laptops is enabling us to look across to mobile app distribution for content.

If people start to access content through their browsers, this makes sense, but – equally - it needs to be delivered using Cloud infrastructure. Cloud is excellent for delivering content via a mobile app or through a browser.

KEY POINT – Social Tools

With Cloud Computing we have the possibility of exploiting social tools that allow us to have a global social reach.

We can now get a global social reach for our learning activities that we're pushing through our teams and through our *virtually* connected groups of employees.

As we move to Social and Mobile Learning models and as we move to include them in our learning strategy, social reach is viable. Global social reach allows us to work with geographically distributed teams very efficiently and very effectively. Cloud is our route to do this.

CLOUD COMPUTING – THE SERVICE PROVIDER PERSPECTIVE

Companies that supply Cloud Computing services do so for several reasons. In this section I will examine these more closely.

KEY POINT – To Maximize Benefits for Customers

The question for **Cloud Service Providers (CSPs)** is this: How can we use Cloud for the maximum benefit of our clients?

So, to understand that, let's look first of all at how and why a software company uses the Cloud, which will help clarify why Cloud Computing is attractive to CSPs.

KEY POINT – To Extend Functionality easily (through Modules)

A CSP uses Cloud so that its customers can extend their functionality easily. Many CSPs achieve this by offering modules or levels of higher functionality in their pricing plans. The concept of pay-as-you-go service today is often a question of linking price to functionality. It is quite common to see two levels applied to Mobile Applications. For example: 'Standard and Pro', where the Pro version is more expensive but always comes with extra functionality. Or perhaps they offer a level of service such as Bronze, Silver, Gold and Platinum. So we use

Cloud to *extend functionality*.

KEY POINT – To achieve/ exploit global reach

CSPs also use Cloud to *achieve global reach*, or to bring the world within the reach of the customer. All large CSPs have several data centers and infrastructure that offer total access to applications in the Cloud all around the globe.

In this way, CSPs empower customers and provide IT services to employees wherever they are in the world at the same flexible pricing plan that they pay at home. This delivers a huge saving to the customer in time-to-market, and the ability to operate on a global scale.

KEY POINT – To benefit from new technologies

CSPs deploy Cloud and work with Cloud to *benefit from new technologies*. As new technologies emerge, they can be added to the Cloud service centrally by the CSP for the benefit of all customers. So for example, as **Bring Your Own Device (BYOD)** has become popular with employees, which is where a company allows the employee to use their own smart device to work on, rather than one the company selects for them, the ability to provide the support for a multitude of devices can be easily done by a CSP. The cost to this for an individual organization can be prohibitive. But, a BYOD strategy is really well suited to Cloud Computing. This is an example of how CSP investment in new technology can be delivered at an affordable level and empower all customers with the latest and best emerging technologies in the market.

KEY POINT – New Industry directions

One of the things that's happened in the last five years in terms of technology growth is that much of the development of applications and much of the development of services have happened for Cloud platforms. Desktop development continues but, of course, the majority of growth is in the use of Cloud. So that's driven by a few things, one of which is smart device growth. The use now of smart devices over PCs has driven the development of applications for smart devices, and these are typically deployed using Cloud from mainstream online stores such as Android Playstore and Apple iTunes. This is fueling an increasing investment in Cloud Computing from major IT vendors such as IBM and Microsoft, who have spent billions of dollars in recent years in an attempt to gain a dominant market position. The earlier statement about IT resources moving us all to Cloud in the next few years cannot be underestimated.

New industry directions have driven us to the Cloud in the first place. Now, in our own industry, we have quite a lot of exploration and developments of Massive Open Online Courses (MOOCs), or Vocational Open Online Courses (VOOCs). These two have driven some technology development in our own industry and these are Cloud-based services. The exploration of this type of education resource is going to continue as it hasn't yet found the perfect solution. Several MOOCs have suffered from membership attrition rates or 'churn' as it is called in the Telco industry. This is where a percentage of customers can be counted upon to leave the platform every year. So if 5% of members leave every year, 5% is needed in new members to avoid loss in overall membership numbers. That puts quite a strain on the MOOC, especially if the percentage is above 10%. So there is a long way to go in this delivery model before success is achieved.

KEY POINT – CSPs use Cloud to deliver increasing Business Value
So Cloud Computing from the CSP perspective is all about delivering

these four things. Essentially they all add up to one large collective benefit and that is **increasing business value.** The primary reason CSPs work in the Cloud is to deliver extra business value to customers and it is in the mutual interest of the customer and the CSP to expand the use of Cloud Computing. That will naturally extend to the Corporate Learning and Development industry.

CHAPTER FOUR KEY POINT SUMMARY

E-LEARNING IN THE CLOUD

DEFINITION

The term "Cloud Computing" refers to the On-Demand delivery of IT resources via the internet with pay-as-you-go pricing.

BENEFITS OF THE CLOUD BUSINESS MODEL

Low, ongoing cost.

No infrastructure investment expenses.

Focus resources away from IT to core business.

Flexible usage plans.

Faster time to market and global reach.

E-LEARNING AND SOFTWARE-AS-A-SERVICE

Content creation based in the Cloud.

Management and tracking.

Browsers and mobile applications.

Social tools.

CLOUD COMPUTING – THE SERVICE PROVIDER PERSPECTIVE

To Maximize benefits for customers.

To extend functionality easily (through modules).

To achieve/ exploit global reach.

To benefit from new technologies.

New Industry directions.

CSPs use Cloud to deliver increasing business value.

CHAPTER 5

ONLINE CONTENT CREATION

AT

IBM

WITH

KAREL GEERAERT

IBM Learning and Development Group is one of the largest E-Learning production organizations in the world. A few years ago, they moved a large amount of their E-Learning production to an online content authoring environment. In this interview, I talked with Karel Geeraert, who is the Director of this initiative, about what he had learned going from desktop production to online (Cloud-based) production.

Simon Birt: Hello everybody. Welcome to today's session which is about Online E-Learning Content Creation. I am very happy to welcome Karel Geeraert from IBM. Karel is going to join us to talk about his and his team's experience with Online Content Creation, and how it can save time and money. We are also going to talk about other aspects of Online Content Creation, and the use of it as part of your Content Authoring strategy.

Let me start by saying that I think Online Authoring is an important aspect of Content Authoring. In recent years, Content Authoring Tools vendors have introduced online environments as an alternative to desktop Authoring Tools, so that today, they are an attractive option for developers. Today we'll explore the pros and cons, and look at the context of their use in relation to desktop tools.

So let me introduce our guest today, Karel. Good morning, Karel.

Karel Geeraert: Good   morning,   Simon.   Good   morning,   audience.

Simon Birt: So, Karel is the leader of Learning and Development for Europe for IBM Global Business Services. IBM is one of the biggest producers of learning content today in the world. Karel has been with IBM for the last 12 years. He has been in learning and workforce management for the past 8 of those 12 years, first, as a Learning Business Partner, and in the last four years he has been leading the IBM Learning Development Group in Europe. We have had a long relationship since IBM started using their Online Content Creation tool about three or four years ago. The reason I wanted to have Karel on the call today is because he has a lot of experience of this, not just from the perspective of creating content, but also from the perspective of managing teams around different countries, focusing on tasks, and relating with customers in several geographies. So, I think he has a lot of experience that we can benefit from on today's discussion.

First of all, I will set the context. Then I have some questions that I want to ask Karel to bring out this experience and these ideas.

What does Online Content Creation offer over desktop authoring, and what are the benefits of blending in an online creation environment to your current desktop tool strategy?

That's really what we want to look at in this session. The content creation process really can benefit from moving online.

Content: team based and collaborative with task sharing

First of all, we can start bringing things together in a better environment. We can be collaborative around our content creation, which is something that, depending on the type of content you are creating, really helps you to work more quickly and with more relevant production.

We can also share tasks. That means that we can employ different Subject Matter Experts according to the knowledge we want, other users with appropriate skills and competencies such as Instructional

Designers and Courseware Developers, and unify them all in the same online project environment. Finally we can do the content review online with the client.

Reusable templates and objects in a common library

We also have the ability in an online environment to work with reusable templates and content, and to have it all held in a central library. One of the big challenges when you have content that is being worked-on on the desktop is object control. For example, if you have several developers working on different pieces of content, the discipline around moving that content into a central library is quite hard to maintain.

Sometimes content is in different versions, or it's in different states on different laptops, or different computers, so that it's not centralized. One of the things that the online environment brings to us is its ability to centralize content and templates.

Access Anywhere (Apple Mac users included)

And, of course, one of the big benefits that we often see with online is that browser access means Apple user access. Most of the desktop content creation tools are only available for a Windows environment which does tend to exclude the growing community of Apple users.

Going online, therefore, enables access through the browser, and so your access is much wider-reaching. It also means that, if you are traveling, you just need access to a browser and you can actually log-on to create and review content. Online Content Creation enables access anywhere, anytime, and it includes your important Apple user base.

Saves Time...

Let's now talk about the benefits of some of the Online Content Authoring that we have seen and - referencing the title of the session today - 'How Online Content Creation Saves Time and Money'. Let's see how this works. Really one of the great benefits we've seen is that with faster production comes time savings and higher performance. That is logical.

...and Money

Finally, let's have a look at the finance side of this. We want to save money and do things more quickly. Certainly some savings are achieved through working more quickly because content development is charged hourly. If the production hours are reduced then it is not unreasonable to assume the project price will go down as well. This is about driving wasted time and increasing efficiency, which is evident in Online Content Creation. Furthermore, on the other side of the coin, content producers can get approvals to invoice for their work more quickly when they include the customer review process in their online environment. This last point is a great plus for doing Online Content Production.

Variety of Content Types

We talked before about how Content Authoring is changing, about how Mobile Learning is becoming more important and wide-spread, and how that content is smaller (bite-sized). If we have to create content for mobile users that's not necessarily E-Learning content, can we do this in the same environment if it is online? And how do we create quick bits of content? Perhaps the online environment is a good place for us to do that, as opposed to working on desktop.

Full Audit Record

Another thing that online content brings is the ability to have a total audit record, or the ability to see the entire process captured within one environment. This is as opposed to having bits of the project out on different desktops, and perhaps linking things with email or some form of project management software. Being online enables us to do it all in one environment.

These are some of the benefits of working online that we are going to discuss with Karel.

So, to summarize, what we would expect from Online Content Production is **faster production** mainly from working in teams and managing resources more efficiently. We expect to get **cost savings and faster invoicing** simply because we can produce content more quickly and get approvals faster. We can send invoices for agreed, completed work more quickly as a result.

It also enables us to run a **full audit record** of our work. Incidentally, one other point is that customer satisfaction actually goes up when they are involved in Online Content Authoring as opposed to desktop authoring. Something else to consider. These are just some some of the real benefits that we are seeing from Online Content Creation.

Simon Birt: *Let's now introduce my guest today, Karel Geeraert, who works at IBM and is deeply immersed in the world of producing E-Learning. Karel over to you.*

Karel Geeraert: Hello, and good morning everyone. I am Karel Geeraert. the leader for IBM content development in Europe and I also have peers in America and in Asia Pacific. We regularly meet together, and we provide content development services and technology services as well as translation services. We have been using Online Content Authoring successfully for several years, which brought me into this topic today.

Simon Birt: *So let me start with question one. Can you give us a brief background as to what your team does at IBM?*

Karel Geeraert: Yes, I can. As most of you are hopefully aware, IBM provides end-to-end learning services to its clients, and that goes from demand planning or learning consulting, training needs analysis, content design, content development, training delivery, learning administration, and Learning Management Systems (LMS) reporting. So we do the full learning cycle. We do that both for our outsourced and internal clients. We have a couple of very large corporations that have fully outsourced their learning operations to us; but also, in some other cases, for the shorter projects or smaller projects, we work on a project-by-project basis. We do these types of projects, and it's needless to say, we deliver these services internally to our 400,000 and more employees.

Simon Birt: *Okay. Thank you. Let's look now at the second question: Can you give some insights as to the challenges you were facing before you moved to Online Content Creation, and the sort of things that made you think about moving to Online Content Creation?*

Karel Geeraert: Yes. One challenge we faced while using the tools before we switched to Online Content Authoring is that we found it very hard to manage the availability of our Subject Matter Experts that had to review our work because we needed them to be available at the times that suited us and we had to agree time slot for this. This wasn't easy.

Then we had a couple of clients that not only wanted us to create content, but they wanted us to maintain and update the E-Learning they had developed themselves, as well. In some cases they even wanted to co-develop. This was awkward to manage on the desktop.

It was also about making sure that everyone in the team was always working on the latest version. If you work in a setting where you have to exchange files or packages, you quickly lose track of which is the latest version, and sometimes people update a version that has already been updated.

Another challenge we had was with speed of content production, as you mentioned earlier.

Finally, we wanted to get these challenges solved, while keeping in pace with the fast evolving E-Learning standards and formats, the Mobile Learning platforms that were coming up, Social and Collaborative Learning, etc.

Primarily our need was to involve the client easily and directly in the development process, to have the Subject Matter Experts (SMEs) able to work on the project when it suited them versus when it suited us, and also what we wanted from the solution we were looking for would then leverage and use existing collateral.

Simon Birt: *There are some good points there. But, you maintain a population of desktop developers as well. So, question three: Can you give us some idea of the benefits of having both options available? I say this because I think a lot of people see this in terms of black-and-white. In other words, they should either be creating content online or they should be creating content on the desktop, and that's not necessarily the right way to think about this. Whereas it is more likely that your experience is that there has been online suitability for certain types of projects and then use of desktop for others. What do you think are the benefits of having both?*

Karel Geeraert: Effectively we use both within IBM. We found that desktop is to be preferred if you have physically co-located teams, where the people working on the project take the project from A to Z or, at least for certain and steady periods of time, they work on one particular project versus switching all the time between specialists in certain domains.

Also a consideration to take into account is bandwidth since you are accessing a server. If you have poor connectivity, then you should definitely go for the desktop version. On the other hand, we do prefer the online if you have to get one task done on a certain project by one person and then you want - for instance - some graphical artist's work to be incorporated, and then the next thing is to have some linguistic review done by somebody else. You can much more easily pass work on from one person to another with the online version, and much more granularly on a title.

If you want to work collaboratively with your clients, the online version is definitely the easiest way to go for you. You don't necessarily have to even share packages with your client. The real advantage we also saw from the online version is that we can easily leverage at any moment in time the best expert for a specific task, which dramatically improves the quality.

We can much more easily balance work between the senior content developer and a junior, where we get our senior developers to do the real one-offs, or the most advanced tasks; while, for the juniors, we bring them in where they can leverage the work that has been done by seniors. They can either use templates or continue to do repetitive tasks the seniors have actually initiated, and the advantage is that this way we also increase their skills. That is also a money saver because, obviously, the junior skills are cheaper than the senior skills, so you can have a nice blend. Then, because of the fact that you can switch between tasks, you can really better leverage and balance your resource utilization. Those are some of the things we found to be real advantages with the online version.

Simon Birt: *That's a good point, that last one, about using the right resources for the right aspects of the project, or bringing them into the project at the right times. That helps especially where you have a blend of people with different competencies and experience. Using them at the right moment makes a big difference. Can you provide some idea of the amount and what types of content your team prepares online?*

Karel Geeraert: Yes. For some of our corporate clients, there are really large amounts of content being developed. We have several hundreds of developers worldwide who do this type of work, but even across Europe and America we have a couple of hundred. We primarily focus on highly interactive E-Learning where we found our Online Content Authoring environment to be a great tool with its embedded quizzes. We have lesser demand for mobile content development, but we still have a portion. We use this even for small developments where the client has some pieces that do not follow the AICC and SCORM standards; where their only requirement is to create a standard wrapper; or, up to the very interactive courses where we include some more sophisticated capabilities with all the video, flash, 3D items, etc. It is really a full range of content types where we use our Online Authoring Tool.

Simon Birt: *Okay, good. We talked a little bit about some of the benefits that you have seen with Online Content Creation. Can you tell us if you have seen improvements in the time it takes to create content, and in the way that you manage the creation online?*

Karel Geeraert: Yes, absolutely. So, first of all, there is **very easy license management.** It doesn't require any tool installation on the desktops, which also means that you can switch a license from one person to another.
You can, as I mentioned, **pass on the sub-tasks,** and even go up to some very specific parts of the content page that you can assign to a certain person to develop.

We also found, for instance, that when a source English version is done in India, or the Americas, we can have the **translation** done, and that can be looked at in both languages, either in Asia-Pacific for Asian languages, or in Europe for the European languages, and you don't have to continue to exchange packages.

Another real beneficial element is this: What do you do if **someone becomes ill** and is absent from work? If the content is loaded on somebody's own desktop or laptop, it can get very difficult to get access to whatever was created.

We have had situations where the project was very time-critical, and where we could **develop in 'follow-the-sun'** principle; so having something started in India and then move to Europe, and then move to the Americas, through the time zones during the day, with no interruption.

We particularly saw **enhanced client satisfaction** because of the collaboration. Clients really like that a lot. The fact that they can see how we develop.

We have leveraged the **re-use of templates** a lot for all the work we have done, and then we have only needed minor customization to change some of the flows for different clients. This re-purposing of content also saves a lot of time.

Simon Birt: *That was an interesting point you made about the license management. It's not something that we first think about with Cloud service, but in larger development groups, that is something that can be a major issue.*

We have talked a little bit about this, but let's expand now on how this has been saving time and money. I know it's something that your group is highly focused on because you're often creating content for customers in an outsourced contract environment where the margin between profit and loss is thin. Can you tell us a little bit about how Online Content Authoring has enabled you to reduce production costs?

Karel Geeraert: Yes. So it's a mixture. Because of the possibilities with Online Content Authoring, we were able to **change some of the processes,** and that's where the money-saving comes.

Without the enabling tool it would simply not have been possible. So, for instance, Instructional Designers create the storyboards directly in the tool, and already from that stage our customers can see how the content evolves. But it meant also that Courseware Developers had to **change their mindset**, really not thinking anymore of the sequence of tasks they have to do to get to the end result, but focusing on their tasks and getting them done in the best way before moving the work back to the project manager, where some other tasks can be assigned to them and to others.

We have to think more about that **collaborative way of working instead of linear** and that **creation and re-use of templates** is really a money saver. It is also a **quality improvement** because you can invest much more in having the template well done, error free, and then leverage that well-done template throughout the course.

Simon: *That's a very good point you made there about **Business Process Improvement**.   One of the things with Online Content Authoring we see is that it is not just a case of changing the Content Authoring environment, but it is a way of **changing your thinking** about how you do Content Authoring, as well. The processes around the*

Content Authoring change, part of which you just described. There is also the point about bringing Instructional Designers into the online process and within the Online Content Authoring environment itself. If you do that you can benefit from having an online audit record of the story-boarding and the online review process. These currently sit outside the authoring process in most linear desktop development tools. But there are challenges with that. How do you see those challenges today and then, going forward, what do you think that will look like?

Karel Geeraert: I think one of the challenges that we still see is that it not only requires a mindset-change from our people, but it also requires a mindset-change from our clients. Some of our clients are used to receiving their storyboards in traditional documents for their review and comment. It is not always obvious to, or comfortable for, all clients to move into this process. However, we have seen that where we managed to move them towards that mindset, **results were much better and we had higher client satisfaction**. Likewise for the review process. Some clients really want to have a paper version. That is particularly true if you work with legal people. They seem to be very used to working on Word documents where they review it, print it out, and do their legal markups, which is a bit different than having them redo their comments directly in the tool. The other caveat to be aware of is that as our clients can clearly see a lot of the possibilities we can do while we develop, they tend to ask for a lot of additional things that we have not agreed to in the initial scope and initial requirements. So we have to pay attention that we don't get too much scope creep, or at least that the expectations don't change drastically from where we started. But, in general, we manage that well, and our clients understand that they get what they pay for, and if they make significant changes to the scope they have normally have an associated cost.

Simon Birt: *That touches again on working in different business processes. I have just one last question here. We referred briefly in another session about how we are seeing content changing because we are getting requests for mobile delivery to be considered. How we distribute content with mobile is unavoidably impacting the way that we create content. Have you seen this in your team where you are now creating content for mobile devices and smart devices, and has this grown over the last year or so?*

Karel Geeraert: Yes, we see still lots of demand. My feeling is there are still a number of technology issues that probably hinder the steep growth in mobile. Everybody is looking at it, but some of the technology aspects still need better resolution. I'm really referring to the issue of responsive design and how that needs to be much more embedded because - even on laptops - you have different form factors. Even if you stick with laptops, it's nice if your content can re-size accordingly to your screen. You would not have your screen present the content exactly for a smart phone as you have for a tablet because that is a way too big difference in form factor. The other aspect is that with responsive design we would be creating universal content. There are still lots of features that work on one platform that do not necessarily work on a different platform, and that has nothing to do with Online Content Authoring. It is simply that the standards are not yet ready as they should be. So when you develop this content you need to be very much aware of the limitations of each platform and you need to come to the largest common denominator.

Simon Birt: *Thank you, Karel, for joining us today. It just remains with me to wish everybody a good weekend, and happy content creation. Thank you all for joining us.*

SIMON BIRT

CHAPTER 6

ON-THE-JOB-TRAINING

AT

FRITO-LAY,

(A PEPSICO COMPANY)

WITH

MARVIN MULLINS

Simon Birt: *Good morning, everyone. Today's session is about On-the-Job-Training. Here to talk about this subject with me is Marvin Mullins from Frito-Lay, which is a part of PepsiCo. Frito-Lay is the division of PepsiCo that manufactures, markets and sells corn chips, potato chips and other snack foods.*

I am very pleased to welcome Marvin Mullins, who works in the Field Training and Development area for Frito-Lay. Marvin has a very interesting job running Field Training for the sales team. Sales Field Training is one of the most important and also the most popular application for On-the-Job-Training, according to many surveys available today.

We are very lucky to welcome Marvin.

Marvin Mullins: Hello, I'm glad everyone's joined us; and, Simon, thank you so much for the opportunity to be with you today.

Simon Birt: *Thank you very much for joining. I look forward to talking with you in a few minutes.*

On-the-Job-Training seems to be one of the hot topics currently in discussion across the Learning and Development industry. However, I should say up front that this session is not a comprehensive view of On-the-Job-Training. You will see that I have structured our session around some themes, and we'll focus on those. Marvin will contribute based upon his experience, on what he has seen, and what he has learned with On-the-Job-Training in a real application in a very large organization.

To begin with I have a definition to set the context for the session.

Definition

On-the-Job-Training (OJT) is teaching the skills, knowledge and competencies that are needed to perform a specific job within the workplace and work environment.

The key point to pick out from this definition is that it's about teaching people how to do their jobs **within their job environments**. It's about teaching skills, knowledge and competencies to do the job at hand. Then it's about applying them or using them in practice within the work environment. This is really what separates On-the-Job-Training from theoretical training or any other type of compliance-based training, such as E-Learning, where you're not necessarily taking what you're learning and applying it straight away.

Another difference is that On-the-Job-Training implies that you are learning or acquiring a knowledge as you're doing it, or 'Learning by Doing'.

There are lots of challenges to effective On-the-Job-Training and the 3 key ones are:

1) What is the appropriate content? In terms of what can be delivered, how do we deliver it, and how do we create it?

2) How do we get it to our employees in an immediate and timely fashion?

3) What is the right technology? Effective On-the-Job-Training can only be delivered if you have the right technology. If not, it's going to be a lot harder to achieve your goals and be effective.

Simon Birt: *Marvin, can you tell us what you do within your job at Frito-Lay? Just set the scene for us so that we've got a view of your work and what your key goals are please.*

Marvin Mullins: Thank you, Simon. I'm on the Learning and Development team. We have several thousand folks that are our clients, ranging all the way from the employees that take our products into the stores and stock the stores (so every place you go you will see some Frito-Lay product), to the next level, which is their supervisors, all the way up to our senior leadership.

Simon Birt: *How long have you been doing this, Marvin?*

Marvin Mullins: I have been in Frito-Lay for 28 years and I have been in this role for the last 7 years.

Simon Birt: *Can you tell us about how your content has changed over the years?*

Marvin Mullins: Sure. Previously, before I joined the team, our On-the-Job-Training was based on traditional instructor-led courses.

Once the new-hire started working out in the market, he or she had a peer-to-peer coach. We have moved from that. The challenge for us was to keep the training consistent. In our peer-to-peer training program there were several thousand employees in the market to train, and a couple of thousand trainers training new hires. Keeping track of what training was going on, or how consistent the training was, became an issue for us to manage. Furthermore, the training wasn't being tracked in those days. To correct these issues would have involved bringing employees out of the market and back to the classroom, which was untenable.

We recently acquired the ability to deliver some of the learning to the field staff because we have invested in digital books, iPhones and iPads for the front line. That has opened up an opportunity for us, and we've moved from traditional Instructor-Led Training (ILT) and paper-based training to where everything we do now is electronic. So no more paper. We do still have a mixed approach, though. We have ILT for some of it to teach principles and so forth, but the On-the-Job-Training is all done through, or supplemented via, a mobile device.

Simon Birt: *So, what you're using now is a blend of different types of approaches to getting the job done?*

Marvin Mullins: Yes. We use traditional Instructor-Led Training as the employee first comes into the organization, and that's just to provide the employee some context about our culture, the overview of their job, etc. Then, once they get into their On-the-Job-Training, we use video to show functional skills that they might need. It's a way for them to see how to put together a display, for instance, or what the shelf should look like. Where, for example, do the Barbecue Lays go, as opposed to the Funyuns or Doritos? We have specific places where we want each of those products on the shelf. Now we have technology where the person servicing the store can pull that plan up in-store. Then, the employee knows where each of the products should go.

Another benefit we get from this approach is it is very helpful for us to leverage the content as a resource, where it almost acts as a tutor for them. Today the peer-to-peer coach is gone, but the need hasn't. The employee is still new. For example, maybe they've been in their role for a month or so, and are out in the store by themselves. They can now use the training content as a resource if they've forgotten something that they had learned previously. They can refer back to it and refresh their learning.

With Mobile Learning, some of the challenges we had in the beginning were that we tried to use E-Learning content, or an ILT course. There were some challenges we faced where it just didn't work. We tried to repurpose what we already had and deliver it into the mobile world, but it just didn't work for a multitude of reasons.

One of the challenges we had is that many of our E-Learning courses ran 15 minutes to 1 hour long. Trying to deliver that into the field where someone is in a supermarket trying to learn a job didn't work. It took too much time. We had to start considering the length of the content. We also had to start considering that learning really doesn't happen as we had traditionally been doing it; bringing someone to our classroom and fire-hosing them. Learning in the field is not going to happen that way. People just don't have the time.

We have a business that's very dynamic. Our employees service multiple stores, so training has to be about quick-learning. We've taken a whole different approach to address this, which is Just-In-Time Learning. Now, we 'chunk' the content into small pieces so our Mobile E-Learning is no more than 3 to 6 minutes long.

Simon Birt: *When your employees are in the store, there's an opportunity to use some of the content that you have to educate store owners and members of the companies you're working with in the supermarkets. Do you do that at the moment, or is that something you're thinking of?*

Marvin Mullins: We leverage the mobile devices, iPads and iPhones to provide information to the store, to the decision-maker. It's not really a learning activity; it's more information-sharing. But you're right, that's available on these devices as well.

Simon Birt: *Good. Now let's move on a little bit into the next area, which is about **Immediacy and Timeliness.** In On-the-Job-Training the principle of **Delivery-on-Demand** is really what separates it from other types of content-based training.*

KEY POINT - On-the-Job-Training

Immediacy and Timeliness for all employees, even those that can be difficult to reach, providing an uninterrupted service.

With On-the-Job-Training, it's about being able to deliver content to people *when* they need it. People need to see the relevant content as they have *the question*. They actually learn at that point, rather than make a note of it, and come back to it much later. Sometimes, because of distractions, they won't always do that. The employee may never come back to that learning opportunity, follow through, and acquire the knowledge, competency or whatever it was that they had the question about at the time. So delivery *on-demand* is what makes On-the-Job-Training effective. If you can deliver the content, or have a system where you are delivering the content, *on-demand,* that's going to be essential.

That naturally leads into *reach,* which today, is about being effective across the globe. In other words, can we *standardize* our On-the-Job-Training specifically so that someone in Asia can be getting the same content (maybe localized), but essentially getting the same learning lessons as they would be getting in North America? Can we design a system to deliver that standardized content to globally dispersed and difficult to reach employees as well? Sometimes, when employees are out and about, they're not able to get to a hot-spot. They may be out in an area where they are relying on their smart devices on a mobile network, and they're difficult to reach. We need to decide whether to use mobile to download content versus using streaming.

Finally, the point that's often forgotten is that the content always has to be available This is successfully addressed with delivery by Cloud. This is about being able to create systems that support learning no matter where or when one is in the world.

For job training to be effective, it should be able to take advantage of the *search* for content. It's almost like a Google effect where you can Google anything, anytime, and you'll get the response to the questions you have. We don't have that in our mainstream corporate systems yet; we don't have that ability to just search on content, pull it up from our learning repository, and then start to learn from that.

That's what we should be aiming towards. Immediacy and Timeliness is really what separates this type of training from other types of training.

Simon Birt: *Marvin, I wanted you to talk a little bit about this now. In the transition from Instructor Led Training to today where the employees in the field are relying on technology to deliver content to them in the store, how have you been able to deliver the content so that it is available as they need it, versus them catching up with it later on?*

Marvin Mullins: We previously did not have a sales force equipped with mobile devices. Now that we do, we can deliver content for them [in the field]. The platform that we're using allows the employee to have content on his or her device *without* streaming. We tried streaming initially. The biggest challenge was that, when the person was in store, the device would lose signal. We were able to come up with a platform where the Mobile Learning, the videos and the other content that are on the server actually get downloaded. The user can go and search what's available for them [in the library] and pull it down onto the device. When they are in the market, in a store, we don't have to worry about connectivity or about increasing data usage charges because it pulls the content down to the device. If they decide that they don't need that content any longer, they can actually take if off the device. Then at any time they choose, they can bring it back down again. We have downloads that are 30 seconds to a minute to deliver and we've been able to reduce that time, because now, the content is short.

The other thing that I haven't mentioned before is that we are able to develop content in-house. The platform that we are using allows us to specialize, or to filter, the kind of content that each individual employee, or groups of employees, gets. So the person that's servicing the store opens an app that's branded Frito-Lay. He or she will see a different set of content than his or her supervisor. We are able to provide different content that is tailored specifically for a person who's doing a particular job, and that really gives us some flexibility.

We started slowly with just a small group and now we have several thousand users in the market using Mobile Learning "Just-In-Time." That is content that's available to the user whether it's Mobile Learning or video. It is about empowering the learners to choose when they need to have content, and then to be able to get it. As you said, Timeliness and Immediacy.

For supervisors and any level above, we provide some leadership content. With this, they actually use the device and Mobile Learning to coach their team members to build their capability.

Simon Birt: *We talked about being able to get feedback, and track and monitor learning activity. Now, I imagine you have seen a change in that, as well as delivering Just-in-Time content. You have also been able to improve your tracking and monitoring. Can you tell us how effective that is now, and what kind of data you are getting?*

Marvin Mullins: Yes. Our challenge previous to having a mobile device was we actually weren't able to track very well. We were counting on post-certification surveys that had a low response rate. Today, once they complete an E-Learning or Mobile Learning course, or even a video (we are even able to see what videos are being leveraged), all the learners have to do on their devices is simply click that they have completed this course. It sends a feed over to our Learning Management System where we are now able to build a learning record of that employee, beginning from when they first came to the organization, on everything they have ever learned. Previously, we were only tracking ILT courses. It's really taken us to a much higher level. We have eliminated paper entirely. For our folks in the front-line market we don't use paper at all, and I'm very excited about it. This has happened within the last two years. We're now able to see what courses or content the learner is actually participating in and create a record for them.

The second thing that the tracking allows us to see is whether or not we're getting much participation in a particular module. We regularly need to assess if a module is delivering value to the learner. If not, then we can remove those modules that aren't. This is a secondary benefit of tracking, which is proving valuable to us.

Simon Birt: That's good to hear because I often discuss tracking and measurement for On-the-Job-Training with customers and hear, "Yes, I can track E-Learning, but On-the-Job-Training is not being tracked." There is not a complete record for the employee of what learning has been completed either. As an employee, one can often feel short-changed, especially if one has to show a record of continuous informal learning for compliance purposes or for certification purposes. So, in the field, if you can track and manage On-the-Job-Training using mobile technology, then you can move to a point where you have a complete record of learning.

The employees would be a lot happier with this approach because they could account for continued learning in the field and actually demonstrate a record of that for an audit. For managers, an audit record can be gathered for each employee, leading to complete tracking of learning in the organization.

KEY POINT – On-the-Job-Training - Technology

Technologies supporting On-the-Job-Training are: Mobile servers and devices, LMS, Content Authoring, Video, Gaming and Gamification, Social Networks, Virtual Reality, Google Glass-type devices, Other Haptic devices, etc.

Now the final theme is around technology. You've mentioned using mobile devices several times. Let's explore what is currently available and what we can do with it. We can deliver an LMS, and we have Content Authoring. We can deliver Mobile Learning, and using social media we can support some Social Learning. We have Enterprise

Social Networks now in many companies and we can deliver Social Learning programs. We have smart devices and mobile applications which are liberating for us to use when mobile.

As regards video, you have talked a little bit about streaming versus download. That's a very important point to work out: whether you think it's practical to deliver streaming or whether you should just go to quick downloads. Clearly streaming can be a challenge. Very often in countries where connection to a good broadband and signal is going to be an issue, this isn't possible.

The development of technologies supporting Gaming and Gamification: this is an area that's set to boom. I saw some figures recently that said that Gaming and Gamification will move from something like $4 billion to $7 billion market by 2017. So, we're at $4 billion today, and it's going to go up to about $7 billion. That's a huge amount of growth forecast for purpose-led gaming for business purposes.

The use of technology to replace apprenticeships, or to replace the experienced peer, while you are learning on the job is attractive. On-the-Job-Training traditionally was done by working with someone more experienced as you work. As we've heard today, technology is replacing this approach.

There is a bright future for Virtual and Augmented Reality software in On-the-Job-training. Immersive technologies that offer a learning experience are going to grow. There are good hardware solutions becoming available, such as Oculus Rift and Google Glass, and the 3D world in general is becoming more mainstream.

Simon Birt: *Marvin, can you talk to us about technologies that you think of being effective today and those that you may be considering for the future?*

Marvin Mullins: We use an E-learning Authoring Tool that makes it easy for us. We develop in-house. We have previously tried going out to vendors for content, but that was too time-consuming and expensive. So we've actually used the Content Authoring Tool to develop our short training courses in-house. In the future, some of the things that we would like to explore are Virtual and Augmented Reality, Gamification and Social Learning. Our organization is very traditional so we haven't done a lot of that yet, but these are the areas we would like to get into. That's where we are going, but again we are very excited about the journey we've had so far and the progress we have been able to make in such a short period of time.

Simon Birt: *Thank you. I did have a question about the LMS that you're using. Is this a Pepsi LMS, or is it one that you deployed at Frito-Lay? How is the LMS strategy working within Pepsico?*

Marvin Mullins: It is a PepsiCo LMS. We purchased it and it is deployed world-wide. The system we are currently using works so well that our sister-company in Canada just recently began using the same platform with iPads and iPhones and [they are] leveraging some of the training that we've got. The content on the device is hosted by a third party mobile server and then it's pushed over to our LMS.

Simon Birt: *Thank you very much for clarifying that. The emerging technologies that we've talked about are definitely becoming more and more mainstream. The key thing is that no one technology satisfies every need; so, as with everything, use the best technologies available to* *support your On-the-Job-Training requirements. It is clear that in an On-the-Job-Training program it is wise to use a combination of technologies.*

The themes that I talked about today with Marvin were: What type of content is appropriate content? How can we deliver that with immediacy and timeliness? And how quickly can we get it to people as they need it?

I would like to thank Marvin who has been a font of knowledge for us today.

Marvin Mullins: Thank you.

Simon Birt: *And thank you, everybody, for joining.*

CHAPTER 7

GETTING STARTED

WITH

SOCIAL LEARNING

WITH

SIMON BIRT

Simon Birt: The session today is 'Getting Started with Social Learning'.

What is Social Learning? Let's have a couple of definitions of this and then look at them in detail.

There's a definition that comes from Bandura Social Learning Theory that **Social Learning is defined as learning through observing others' behavior, attitudes and outcomes of those behaviors.**

Social Learning is not therefore done in isolation. The learning comes from each other and from watching behaviors. Social Learning naturally leans towards socially driven activities and characteristics.

What is Social Learning enabled by today? Well, Social Learning in its purest sense has been around for a long time. We've all learned from each other, as children to adults, as we grow up. Social Learning is something we do every day, and we are naturally all socially capable of learning from each other. It is in our nature. But, when we define Social Learning within Learning and Development, what we've been talking about is technology-enhanced Social Learning. **This means learning that's enabled by social networks, social media, mobile** devices or smart phones, the internet and the Cloud.

HOW IS SOCIAL LEARNING APPLIED?

Social Learning is mainly used for sharing knowledge among employees. Studies have shown that social networks enable faster employee connections, speed up access to answers from colleagues who have questions posted in them, and improve performance.

KEY POINT - Social networks are intrinsic to building up trust among employees in the workplace.

Connecting to colleagues who are experienced and knowledgeable is easier in social networks than in email, for example, and this helps to build trust and confidence among employees.

KEY POINT – Social Learning underpins working with other employees (collaborating).

An excellent way to get exercises and projects going in the network is to use collaborative Social Learning. This is a readily accessible and quite simple way to use Social Learning as part of your strategy.

KEY POINT – Social Learning is excellent for building your career and job support networks.

When you get into an organization, one of the most important things that you can do is to connect to people who can help you with your role or help you with your career. Using Enterprise Social Networks internally enables you to do that very efficiently.

Extending this to **employee mentoring** is also a useful way of leveraging Enterprise Social Networks for Learning and Development. Mentors can collaborate with many more employees using Enterprise Social Networks than they can in face-to-face meetings. Although, a blend of both is optimum.

KEY POINT – Social Learning is an intrinsic part of 70:20:10.

This is the idea that 70% of learning is focused on Learning Through Experience, 20% is focused on Learning Through Others and 10% is focused on Learning through Courses and Programs. Social Learning is essential to the first two areas and can contribute to the third.

KEY POINT – Social Learning supports On-the-Job-Training.

Social Learning is immediate and timely, so it's very fast for employees to get answers from colleagues about problems. For example, imagine if you are in the field at a customer site or at your place of work and you have an urgent question. You can normally get an answer more quickly from your colleagues if you post it to your social network than if you use email. This is simply because a post in your social network is an invitation for an answer from *any* employee, or group, and email is targeted to a smaller number, any of which may be unable to answer at that time. Also, you can post links to content that helps people get tasks done. For example, instructional videos and .pdfs. Posting links provides a very quick way to share content with your network.

KEY POINT – Social Learning is an excellent way to do mentoring and talent development.

Social Learning is a great way to make mentors available who aren't normally available except to a small group of people who've been selected for fast-track development. It can affect a small number of people because you just don't have the access to the person doing the mentoring. And very often mentoring is either one- to-one or one-to-few. When you have Social Learning or a social network at your disposal, you can increase that mentoring reach dramatically. You can now put the person who has the knowledge and who's doing the mentoring at the center of a series of mentoring activities, and you can have many people connected in the social network. You can expand a mentoring and talent development program by a very large number.

KEY POINT - Social Learning is very good for building culture and sharing experience.

Building a corporate culture using your social networks where your Social Learning process is central is a very good way to share policies and ideas that form your culture. Other cultural activities, such as social event programs, can be highly effective when run via the social network.

KEY POINT - Social Learning is also part of a blended strategy.

It's an excellent way for you to deliver a thread, or a channel, of your learning strategy in tandem with other learning methods. In a blended learning program, Social Learning supports knowledge-sharing, workplace learning, collaborative learning, and many other important learning activities.

It's true that Social Learning is a relatively new phenomenon. In the last few years, many organizations have experimented with it and it is now considered a mainstream form of corporate learning. In the next few years Social Learning will become a greater piece of the learning blend.

KEY POINT – Social Learning is excellent for consensus gathering.

If you have an internal social network deployed, it's an excellent mechanism for you to do consensus gathering when you're working with large numbers of people online at the same time. For example, an employee might post a problem, a question, or a dilemma, and then a number of people for whom the subject is relevant will be able to respond giving ideas and answers in return. This has been called 'crowd-sourcing' when used in social media. Normally, there would be a consensus gained towards the end of that activity of the key ideas leading to a shortlist for consideration. It can be excellent when you've got teams working together towards a common goal where consensus gathering is a critical component of this process.

Consensus gathering is also excellent for getting feedback, or survey-type information, from members of your organization as to how they feel about a particular policy or how they are learning an activity. So it's a very good way of doing **barometer-like check ups,** like taking the temperature of the organization at a particular moment.

KEY POINT – Social Learning is supportive of On-Boarding.

For new recruits, on-boarding with Social Learning offers programs and exercises where new employees are challenged to connect to other employees that can help them build their corporate network . New recruit on-boarding really does benefit from the use of social networks for connecting and knowledge sharing. It's also an excellent place to *start* with Social Learning in your organization.

KEY POINT – Social Learning is effective for Sales Support.

Another good area is in the sales team. We all know that continual effort is spent on training sales people to guide and generate more business for their organizations. One of the big challenges for a sales team is to manage a partner network. For example, if there are partners and agencies that have to be managed and trained, one of the things that partner sales people have to do is to keep them up to date with product information, and to train them on updates. So if they connect the partners into the social environment, it is an excellent way to help teach and train the extended sales network.

ENSURING SUCCESSFUL SOCIAL LEARNING

Successful Social Learning implementation is not just about deploying Enterprise Social Networks, though. Everybody who's been involved in social business understands that there's a behavioral change required to get success with Social Learning.

KEY POINT – Large-scale Participation.

One of the big things you need is large-scale participation. Ideally, you need all employees to participate in this. Equally, one can't take an employee who doesn't intuitively participate in the Enterprise Social Network and train them using Social Learning. They will need to be trained to use Social, and then an active coaching program to reinforce the training is often required. So you really must encourage people to take part in Social Learning and support employees with the right training. That's a central point of running a successful Social Learning program.

KEY POINT – Identify Clear Programs or Projects.

It's a good idea to have clear programs or projects to start out with. When you start to motivate people and build up momentum around your Social Learning program, it's a good idea to have very clear goals to gather everyone around and a set of exercises ready to go. In this way, as you get everybody excited about doing Social Learning, you can drive a relevant learning project through with it. This will energize employees constructively because they will see that they have got to change behavior in an applicable sense to their work.

KEY POINT – Scaffolding is important.

Definition:

Scaffolding refers to a variety of instructional techniques used to move learners progressively toward stronger understanding and, ultimately, greater independence in the learning process. The term itself offers the relevant descriptive metaphor: trainers provide successive levels of temporary support that help learners reach higher levels of comprehension and skill acquisition that they would not be able to achieve without assistance. Like physical scaffolding, the supportive strategies are incrementally removed when they are no longer needed, and the trainer gradually shifts more responsibility over the learning process to the learner.[2]

Scaffolding is important in Social Learning. As mentioned above, everybody has to participate. But not everybody naturally understands what they need to do, or how to take part in Social

_____

2 Definition taken from The Glossary of Education Reform created by the Great Schools Partnership, with thanks (http://edglossary.org/scaffolding/)

Learning. If you think of the people that blog in your organization, you may recall that not everybody blogs. In fact, there are commonly only a few who are really enthusiastic bloggers . Social Learning can be the same. You can find that there are people in the community that are extremely active around Social Learning, but that others are really just sitting on the sidelines.

What we need to do when we try and drive a Social Learning program is to scaffold people so they all have the same skill set and understanding. One way to do this is by working in communities. We'll get small groups of people, normally the enthusiasts first, and task them to create a small nucleus within the organization where they start to spread the word and build out enthusiasm and interest in Social Learning among their colleagues. And, as I've said before, you need a project to give this some purpose. So your early scaffolders will actually drive adoption with the project. Then you progress to larger scale communities [of scaffolders] until, before you know it, you have actually got your whole organization, in one form or another, connected into your social network, doing your Social Learning. Whether this learning is external on Twitter or other social media, or whether this is on internal Enterprise Social Networks, the same rules apply. You still need to have the same scaffolding support to get people to take part in Social Learning.

NEW ROLES FOR SOCIAL LEARNING

So this means we've got **new roles for learners and trainers**. There are a lot of new roles that start to pop-up when a company starts really driving behind the Social Learning strategy.

KEY POINT – Social Learning Managers.

We find, for example, that we need Social Learning Managers in our organization. For those of us in L&D who might not be aware of what Social Learning Managers do, the Social Learning Manager takes on the responsibility for driving the Social Learning programs. Creating the Social Learning programs in consensus with the Learning and Development team as part of a blended learning strategy is a key focus of this new role. So I encourage you to look at your E-Learning programs, your Mobile Learning programs. Look at any other type of classroom or web-based conferencing that you're doing, and then tie-in Social Learning to support that. In this way, Social Learning is a continuation, or at least it's an important contributing piece, of what you're doing in the 'big learning picture'. Perhaps Social Learning can be used to repeat and reinforce other training. But, as it's driven through the Social Learning programs, it becomes a different way of reinforcing what you're trying to achieve with other types of training. Put together with that training, it is a much more effective approach.

KEY POINT - Community Managers.

Community Managers are a very important new role in organizations today. Community Managers are employees that are naturally social in their work. They intuitively want to help other employees acquire social working skills and get the confidence they need to start driving the community to work. So, Community Managers are essential.

Community Managers - and interestingly enough I've spoken to a lot of them - have different views on policing, or moderating, at the beginning of a new Social Learning program. They don't all have the same view about what their role is in this area. Some think that they're there to monitor or watch *the content* that is being shared and then to police it. Other Community Managers have a view that they can be more relaxed about what's being shared because what's more important is that people are actually sharing. They argue that they don't want to shut down people just when they start to get confident with sharing knowledge for the sake of policing the content. They want to encourage employees to share at first. The content errors can be addressed later.

KEY POINT – Social Coaches.

Following on from that, one might then think about having Social Coaches as well. Community Managers look after the communities as a whole, and then we have Social Coaches. Social Coaches will assist people who have problems in understanding about how to participate, where to participate, and what the right sort of content to share is. Social Coaches can help with these challenges.

KEY POINT – Early Adopters and Social Stars.

Let's not forget the early adopters and the social stars in your organization. These are employees that quite instinctively take to working with Social Learning, enthuse their colleagues to participate, and love working in the social environment. Do not necessarily create a new role for that person, but add it to what they already do, and ask them to maybe take a more participatory role in your Social Learning program.

And, of course, when we talk about Social Learning, particularly when we talk about training, it all sits within the Learning and Development Department area of responsibility. However, Social

Learning has non-professionally developed, employee-made content addressing informal corporate learning needs. You should start to involve people from other parts of the organization in supporting roles, and you should not just be concerned with getting your trainers or other Learning and Development people involved. If you can recruit other members of your organization to support you in this within their *own* departments, it will significantly increase the chances of success.

SOME POINTERS TO SUCCESS.

So now, let's talk about a few helpful tips to help you understand the sorts of things that can make a **Social Learning program successful**.

KEY POINT – Top-Down Engagement.

First of all, it's imperative to have top-down engagement. In fact, it's worth repeating. It is critical that you have top-down engagement, and by that I mean you have the CEO and senior managers who understand the value of driving social programs and are interested in pushing Social Learning. Because companies that already have an Enterprise Social Network deployed will have employees actively engaged in social roles, you can assume there's a fair deal of buy-in and support for Social Learning. There is no doubt it should be easier to engage Social Learning in a company that has already deployed tools and policies to support social business. However, whether yours is practiced or new to social business, these tips will help.

KEY POINT – Maintain a Light Touch.

Don't over-police or discourage people when they start to share content. Empower them to do it, but then guide them. One way to do this is to **create rules of the road**. It's important to let people understand that there's a community plan or Social Learning Policy. It governs appropriate behavior, what content is sensitive and should not be shared, and what sort of checks-and-balances there are for making sure that things are happening appropriately. You might have a procedure in place for arbitrating between departments, for example. So create rules for the road. Make everybody aware of what they should be thinking of when they work socially.

KEY POINT – Develop a Coaching Program.

A coaching program is always helpful. Coaching others to adopt correct behaviors is essential. So, when you develop your Social Learning program, don't just think about what it is you're trying to achieve from a learning perspective. Think also about how you're going to help and support employees to acquire their skills and competencies. As I said earlier, make sure you have your social stars in place and your social coaches to support other employees.

KEY POINT – Recognition and Reward Schemes.

And then design rewards and promote. A lot of social networks these days come with the ability to promote some sort of social badging. These are there so you can promote good social behavior through rewards. You can identify and recognize stellar employees with certain badges and rewards. Rewards make employees understand that they are achieving the right levels of behavior, and promoting their success within the social network tells their colleagues about it for them to learn from. If people post something that has been particularly useful, some content that's particularly helpful to other employees, for example, then promote that and publicly recognize them.

TECHNOLOGY

KEY POINT – Learning Planning.

So first of all, it's very important when you start large blended plans that have Social Learning, Mobile Learning, and E-Learning that you're doing Learning Planning. Learning Planning is a tool which enables employees to create their own learning plans. Within those learning plans employees can register large numbers of different types of content, so that they can see whether they're doing a Social Learning program, or an E-Learning program or Classroom training, for example. But Social Learning can definitely be accommodated.

KEY POINT – Content Authoring.

Social Learning Content Authoring can be done with a number of Authoring Tools that are available today. These are tools that enable you to create content and post it socially. They are essentially created for the everyday user who would regularly work with Microsoft PowerPoint, but then would enhance it using these tools, and post that enhanced content to share it.

KEY POINT – Content Management.

Content management: you need to be able to manage your content as always. You *can* use your Learning Management System; but, if you don't have an LMS and you're starting new to this, then find one which can hold SCORM content for learning tracking <u>as well as</u> all types of other content such as MP4, MP3 and .PDFs. These types of 'informal content' are always present in Social Learning, and your LMS should support them. Furthermore, support should be available for XAPI or 'Tin Can', as it is sometimes called, which is a new standard for tracking learner behavior. Having all your content hosted in one place is important for security and curating. Being able to track results, to track things like usage, access and status of completion of your learners is also important to Social Learning.

KEY POINT – Mobile Distribution.

Mobile distribution is next. When we're talking social we're talking about getting content on our phones and our tablets. So again, mobile distribution is very important. Deploying a Mobile Server is exactly how you would manage that type of content. You can deliver all the types of content you need to from your mobile device. Instead of .pdf's, you can deliver Mp4s and Mp3s. You can also deliver SCORM content, so a wide range of different types of content are supported; and, of course, you'll be accessing your social network from your mobile device as well.

KEY POINT – Enterprise Social Networks.

Let's talk briefly about other technology. I'll start with Enterprise Social Networks. This refers to products like IBM Connections, Microsoft Yammer and Jive. These are Enterprise Social Networks that would be deployed enterprise-wide by an organization for employees to use as their digital workplace. They are gradually replacing many of the tasks that used to be done by email.

An Enterprise Social Network is not a product learning companies would sell, although some learning companies have developed social networks in their products. Typically though, this is a strategic piece of software that is bought by the organization's IT Department as infrastructure. Many Authoring Tools produce content that will work with your social network; so, whatever you have, will normally fit in because the Social Learning content can be posted to and accessed from any social network.

KEY POINT – Social Media.

Social media is also an option for Social Learning, of course. There's a limit to what you can do with Social Learning in Social Media, although I know a lot of people have tried to develop programs using it. Something like **LinkedIn** is an external Business2Business social network that offers a good way to post content for knowledge-sharing, and it gives employees some experience of how to work with Social Learning.

Twitter allows you to reference various resources around the internet and allows you to make fast check-in/check-out commentaries. Twitter is good for driving some activities, building followers and posting links. It's a good place to build credibility, trust, and to share knowledge.

YouTube is a great place to locate instructional videos. Many companies these days like to have an internal repository for their own learning purposes. They have their learning video content internally on a server in a similar way to You Tube.

Google+ and FaceBook are social networks which are very popular for connecting to friends and family. Both have made a play for the business market but neither has been very successful as Enterprise Social Networks; but, as social media for Marketing and Customer Relations, they have been very widely adopted by businesses. Facebook seems to be the most successful of these and today many companies have their own FaceBook page and accompanying FaceBook strategy.

Games: There are a few repositories available today where communities can access game engines and build games. The most popular of these have a social community attached to them. A good example of this is 3D Unity, which is very usable and popular.

KEY POINT – Social Analytics.

Finally, we see the emergence of Social Analytics. This is an important area of all social engagement and there are several vendors producing viable solutions. The idea with social analysis is that we can get insights to social activity and engagement. Here we can learn about trending topics of discussion and popular themes among social learners. In the future, we hope to influence conversations, or at least place content strategically into the conversation, to gain trust and build consensus, whether it be for a product, a service, political party, or a good cause. Understanding and strategically intervening in social engagement is going to be a huge growth area in the business intelligence market.

SOCIAL LEARNING ADOPTION

So let's now turn to the topic of adoption. One of the big lessons learned from social business in the last three years, and Social Learning as a part of that, is that once the tools are in place to enable and empower participation, adoption is not guaranteed.

How to get users engaged and drive up participation levels is a bigger challenge than deploying technology. It involves behavior change, and that is sometimes tough to engineer.

There are several aids that can be used to help this process and smooth the transition. Here are some ideas:

KEY POINT – Social Learning Workshops.

Number one, look at introducing workshops, and - if possible - tie the social journey to an existing project or budgeted learning activity. For example, if you have a mentoring program due to launch, ensure that you deploy a Social Learning aspect as part of the project. This gives everyone a goal to aim for from the workshops and other activities you are running.

KEY POINT – Trial and Error.

As social is still quite new, there is a trial-and -error element to what you do. Don't be afraid of that. The best social results have often come from bold steps taken. Ensure that you remove as much risk as you can, but essentially let it take wings and encourage all participation, correcting and guiding where needed.

KEY POINT – Recruit and Empower Social Champions.

Recruit social champions and empower them to recruit in their turn,

SIMON BIRT

so that the overall positive momentum spreads quickly. Social champions not only act as catalysts to the Social Learning, but they also provide great community support, whether that be technical in nature, around best-practices, or otherwise. The key point is to let people take up the cause themselves and entrust in them the power to post, make comments, and pass on their knowledge and experience.

<u>CHAPTER SEVEN KEY POINT SUMMARY</u>

<u>GETTING STARTED WITH SOCIAL LEARNING</u>

HOW IS SOCIAL LEARNING APPLIED?

1. Social networks are intrinsic to building up trust among employees in the workplace.
2. Social Learning underpins working with other employees (collaborating).
3. Social Learning is excellent for building your career and job support networks.

WHAT CAN SOCIAL LEARNING BE USED FOR?

1. Social Learning is an intrinsic part of 70:20:10.
2. Social Learning supports On-the-Job-Training.
3. Social Learning is an excellent way to do mentoring and talent development.
4. Social Learning is very good for building culture and sharing experience.
5. Social Learning is also part of a blended strategy.
6. Social Learning is excellent for consensus gathering.
7. Social Learning is supportive of On-Boarding.
8. Social Learning is effective for Sales Support.

ENSURING SUCCESSFUL SOCIAL LEARNING

1. Large-scale participation.

2. Identify clear programs or projects.

3. Scaffolding is important.

NEW ROLES FOR SOCIAL LEARNING

1. Social Learning Managers.

2. Community Managers.

3. Social Coaches.

4. Early Adopters and Social Stars.

SOME POINTERS TO SUCCESS

1. Have top-down engagement.

2. Maintain a light touch.

3. Develop a coaching program.

4. Recognition and reward schemes.

TECHNOLOGY

1. Learning Planning.

2. Content Authoring.

3. Content Management.

4. Mobile Distribution.

5. Enterprise Social Networks.

6. Social Media.

7. Social Analytics.

SOCIAL LEARNING ADOPTION

1. Social Learning workshops.

2. Trial and error.

3. Recruit and empower Social Champions.

SIMON BIRT

CHAPTER 8

GAMIFICATION,

GAMING MECHANICS,

AND

GAMING E-LEARNING CONTENT

AT THE

NHS

(NATIONAL HEALTH SERVICE), U.K.

WITH

RICHARD PRICE

Simon Birt: Our session today is all about Gamification, Game Mechanics, and Gaming E-Learning Content. This is a growing area of study and use in the distance learning industry. Evidence is now available showing that learners who are trained through Serious Games retain content better and for longer. Training which addresses behavioral change has also been boosted by serious gaming, which is proving very effective.

I would like to introduce my guest at this point. His name is Richard Price, and we're going to have an exciting discussion today about how Richard and his team have managed to create an excellent game within an E-Learning Content Authoring Tool which was used to change behavior in the National Health Service (NHS) of the United Kingdom.

Part of the good news from this project was that Richard didn't have to invest in a tremendous amount of technology to get gaming into E-Learning. Richard is going to help us understand how he did it, and how he managed to help address some behavioral changes that his team were looking to address at the Ambulance Service. So I'd like to say 'Good morning' to Richard.

Richard Price: Good Morning, everybody. Good morning, Simon.

Simon Birt: *Good morning, Richard, and welcome. We'll come back to you in a minute.*

As always, I like to set the context for the discussion. I'd like to explain exactly what aspect of Gamification and Gaming we're talking about. There are couple of definitions I'd just like to run through.

First of all, let's talk about **Gamification**. This is a term that's used a lot. From the internet and from social media, there seems to be some consensus on what this term is about.

Definition*:*
Gamification **is the use of game thinking and game mechanics in non-game contexts to engage users [Gamers] in solving problems.**

This definition is a succinct way of summarizing a few of the definitions that you may see. We talk about the use of Game Thinking and Game Mechanics in a non-Game context to engage users in solving problems. And, though it doesn't necessarily have to be used for solving problems, it is particularly good for that. The key point is this: when we talk about Gaming or Gamification, we're talking about using the existing skills, experience and knowledge in the gaming industry and applying that to a non-game context, such as corporate training.

So let's move on and ask, 'What are Game Mechanics?' Let's have a look at this definition.

Definition*:*

Game Mechanics **are constructs of rules intended to produce a game or Game-Play.**

This can include badges, rewards, increasingly hard problem levels, movement through the content according to learner's [gamer's] answers (branching), Fantasy Scenarios, Simulations, etc.

Game Mechanics are constructs of rules intended to produce a game or Game-Play. So what does that mean? Well, it refers to things like including badges, rewards, and having increasingly hard problem levels. So, as the player goes through the stages in a game, things tend to get more complicated and a little more difficult. This is the type of construct the gamer will encounter.

Another construct is movement through the content according to learners' answers, what we typically call in E-Learning 'branching'. According to the gamer's answer, direction is given to the next level, or the next step, or the scenario that's presented. Progress is dependent on the answer and is selected by the game from different predetermined response conditions.

Also common are Fantasy Scenarios. These can be fantasies based on real life experience. They simulate a real customer situation. We can create a real customer service environment to be as life-like as possible where mistakes can be made in a safe environment. In other words, you're not actually in front of the customer, you're gaming through an example of a fantasy.

These could also be Simulations, which are very similar to Fantasy Scenarios. However, a simulation may also include tasks that you're asked to complete. For example, flying an aircraft using a simulator. Simulations make use of Haptic Tools, which are tools that create the interface to the game software and record the tactile use of the tool by the learner. A pilot's joystick would be a good example of this. Simulation also makes use of virtual and augmented reality models within the game.

So, this is the area of Game Mechanics. Now let's move on to ask what's meant by Game Thinking.

Definition*:*

Game Thinking **is orienting oneself to look at a piece of E-Learning content from the perspective of a game designer [not an Instructional Designer].**

For example, learners become players; players are central to the game; players have a sense of control over the game; players are playing rather than learning; and players take risks safely.

Designers should orient themselves to look at learning content from the perspective of a game designer. Game Thinking is about considering how to create content for a player. For example, learners become players. They're not E-Learners anymore. It's helpful to think of them that way. Players are central to the game and the content is there to respond to their actions, which is often different to the way a learner engages with E-Learning.

Players have a sense of control because the player in a game has a sense of autonomy and is in charge of the game. He or she is the central character. Everything that happens in the game is a consequence of either an action or response that the player makes.

We create safe environments where players can take risks because that's how they learn without real penalties. They are allowed to take those risks without the consequences that they would encounter in real life.

And finally, of course, games are fun. It's very important that we accept that games are designed to be fun even as they address serious topics. They're designed for learners to enjoy, and therefore we've got to keep the fun element in all of the games that we create.

Now let's talk about 'Gaming Your Learning'.

Definition:

Games-for-Learning are referred to as 'Serious Games'. A Serious Game is a game designed for a primary purpose other than entertainment.

What are the key benefits of using Gamification in learning and training?

1) We've known now for some time that we get higher learner engagement and increased satisfaction when we use Serious Games.

2) Gaming has the potential to change behaviors, which addresses the Kirkpatrick levels 3 and 4, for those of you familiar with the Kirkpatrick Training Evaluation Model (see chapter 9). This is very important because it's not just a training event in the way that E-Learning or classroom training is. Gaming actually impacts the way people think and the way they work. It is normally high in problem solving challenges. We can get the kind of results that follow through into the work place as a result of building Gamification into E-Learning.

We can get a bigger impact on **business value** and, of course, all training these days in any organization is about justifying the business value of the training. It's not enough now to do a training event. We want to know that people have actually started to do things differently in the workplace because of training they have received. It's not enough to say that people attended training anymore. It is important to demonstrate that they actually carry through what they learn and apply this in the workplace. Putting Gamification into your learning content is a great way of doing that.

So, now on to using E-Learning tools for gaming. We've talked a little bit about gaming in general and some definitions that apply to that. And we've looked at the benefits of using Serious Games in training.

How do we use an Authoring Tool for gaming? The questions we often hear asked are, "Can Instructional Designers incorporate game design in E-Learning content?" "Do they know how to create game design in the first place?" and, "Can they do it within the technology used for E-Learning?"

Richard is going to address these questions as we go through the conversation today. Richard did a good job with his team creating a scenario and other game-based constructs, to applying Game Mechanics and Game Thinking to E-Learning content.

Simon Birt: *Hello, Richard.*

Richard Price: Hello, Simon.

Simon Birt: Richard created a Serious Game for the National Health Service (NHS) in the U.K. The aim of it was to change the behavior of ambulance crews towards elderly patients. The game was funded in part by an E.U. project called Web Wise. This is something that the E.U. does regularly, just as there are bodies in the U.S.A. such as ASTD that do the same thing. They fund development and research in learning. This was one of the projects that the E.U. funded and the challenge was to create a training game that could help change behavior.

Simon Birt: *My first question for Richard: Can you introduce yourself, and tell us what your role is at the National Health Service and the sorts of training you do?*

Richard Price: Thanks, Simon. Well, I work for The National Health Service in the United Kingdom and it's actually one of the ten largest employers in the world. We're often up there with Indian Railways, the Chinese Army, Wal-Mart and McDonalds. In terms of numbers of employees, we've got over a million doctors, nurses and paramedics employed by us. It's a monumental task to train that many people.

We use E-Learning to support statutory and mandatory training. At one time, I was working with the ambulance service part-time, but now I'm working for them full-time. That's how I got enrolled for this project. We were looking at how we could train round about 4,500 ambulance staff with various games.

Simon Birt: *I imagine that the typical make-up of an ambulance crew is a mix of different types of people?*

Richard Price: That's right, yes. We've got a good mixture of people of different ages and of different abilities in terms of using the technology, as well.

Simon Birt: *Quite a diverse group then. Can you give us some insight as to the challenges you were facing before you created the game, and what sort of things you were thinking about?*

Richard Price: Sure. So in the U.K. - and I'm sure it's no different from the U.S. - we're facing financial challenges in terms of delivering education and training. In the recent past, we've taken ambulance crews off the road for days or potentially weeks at a time to train them. We don't have that luxury anymore. They're employed primarily to save lives; and, if we take them off the road, they can't do that. So we have to look at more innovative ways of training them. Learning Technology has formed a big part of that over the years in terms of supporting what they can do. We train them in their spare time; and, if they have tablets, they sit in a lay-by beside a road where they can be learning through their mobile devices.

We consistently got very good anecdotal feedback from our patients about the care that our crews gave, but our staff have criticized the type of learning that we deliver through our platforms in these sort of words: 'dull, tedious, repetitive'. How do we break that repetitive and dull cycle so that we're making our E-Learning much more interesting? How do we get people motivated? Well, we got involved with a European-funded project called Web Wise, as Simon mentioned. And the idea with that was to explore the use of Web 2.0 technologies to improve learning outcomes. That came along at a very good time because we were already thinking about how we could introduce Gamification into our learning and education. The European project came at just the right time and they actually provided a small amount of money to contribute towards it.

Simon Birt: *Thank you, Richard. Can you describe what your game is, and how it was applied and used?*

Richard Price: Sure. I've got some images to show you so you can have a look at what we produced. The purpose of the learning was really to remind crews of the the importance of good patient care; treating the patients with respect and dignity. In the good old days, we used to call it 'bedside manner'. This is a common complaint that we deal with.

We get it right most of the time. There are occasions when we don't and our patients do not get the care they expect from our staff. We really want to make sure that we address that.

We took the concept of storytelling and getting empathy from users, and then created a 'soap opera'. We tell a story about each of the characters and we introduce them through video clips and other resources that are associated with them. In this way you get to know them as you work through the game.

We created a Facebook page for some of the characters to bring in realism. We provided a back story and scenario. This was all done in our E-Learning tool.

At the beginning of the game, learners are presented with a map. As learners move through the game, we start introducing additional buildings and houses. When people click on those houses they get introduced to a new character.

So, for example, if they click on a community building such as the hospital, they get introduced to some of the characters in the hospital.

We created a town hall and other typical town buildings. We've got a mayor, just like most British towns. He has a Twitter page. He has a Facebook page.

One of the key lessons we learned was to enrich the game with detail. The attention to detail resonated with the learners. These kinds of things make a huge difference. As we introduced all the characters in our scenario to the learner, we had scenarios where they met each other and interacted.

This is all developed as a realistic story, but in the form of a soap opera. It really worked well and all of the learners became immersed in the story in such a way that their real behaviors emerged during the game. This allowed us to influence those behaviors for the better during the course of the game.

Another key element of the game was the introduction of moments of reflection from the different characters. This gave us the opportunity to have the learners examine their behaviors after the interaction and make conclusions for themselves about how correct they were. For example, we introduced follow-up conversations between ambulance drivers and their supervisors which were presented as learning moments about their behavior.

Another example is where an elderly lady reflects on her treatment and her experience by the two ambulance paramedics that responded to her call.

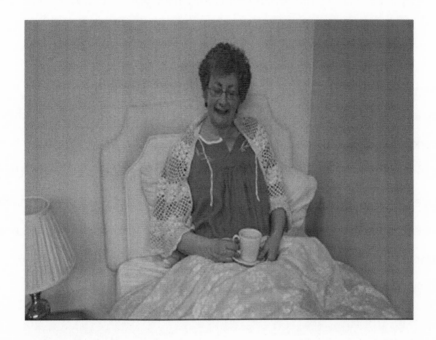

At the end of that, we got to the point where learners were asked to reflect on how they would have behaved differently.

We also encouraged discussion through forums that we used in our Learning Management System. This was another important opportunity to discuss and reflect on the game, and to examine how the interactions had been treated from the aspect of behavior.

Simon Birt: *Tell us a little bit about how you got that interaction going. Did you find that people actually took to it or…?*

Richard Price: It took a bit to get to that point, Simon. It's not an environment where people are used to gaming at their workplace. A lot of people do play games in their spare time, but many don't. It was a challenge just to satisfy the serious gamers that have obviously got a lot of experience and the novices who have never played these games in their lives. So we had to produce a hybrid that allowed us to satisfy both audiences. Equally, the novices had to learn how to game. However, it didn't take long.

Simon Birt: *I'd like to talk about the Game Thinking that you applied. You've talked about characters, the idea of creating a scenario, the idea of presenting simulated conversations with people who are supposed to react the way the public do to the ambulance crews, and other game constructs. What other type of Game Thinking did you apply for Serious Games?*

Richard Price: I don't know if anyone remembers a game from the early 90s called Sim City? I spent probably far too much time in my teenage years playing this, but it's an example of a serious game without the serious learning outcomes. There were lots of serious factors for you to manage as a player. You were having to build buildings, you had to negotiate tax rates - that kind of thing - and lots of factors to manage to keep your residents happy. This is where we got the inspiration for our map idea, as you can see in the picture.

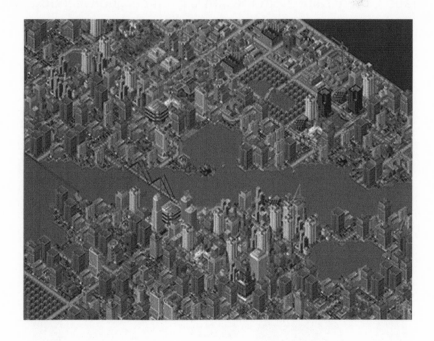

And, you may remember, newspaper headlines popped up during the game that told you about all the sort of events that were happening within the game.

We tried to emulate that so that at the end of introducing some characters we introduced the newspaper popping up to develop the character story further.

This helps to create an immersive environment within the game. Our inspiration, then, came from the Sim City game, and we introduced several elements from the game into ours.

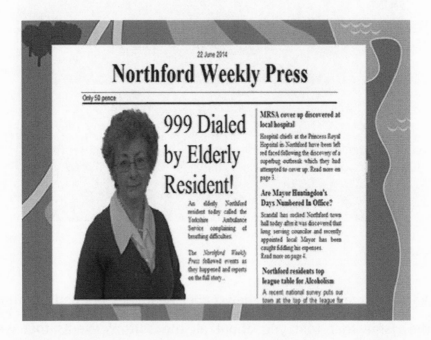

An example of another element we used is unlocking parts of the game according to the player's progress. At several points in the game the learner discovers new buildings, or objects, because they are hidden until unlocked by their progress or action in the game.

Simon Birt: *Thank you, Richard. Can you now talk about the game mechanics? How did you employ these within the game?*

Richard Price: Well, earlier in the session you talked about Fantasy Scenarios. That's one of the game constructs we used. I discussed our scenario earlier, and we tried hard to base it on reality. We did get experts to critique it and make sure that we weren't doing anything that was clinically incorrect. But, we also made sure there was a bit of tongue-in-cheek fun in terms of the way we delivered it. The characters probably weren't as professional as our real staff are, but it was designed to elicit a response from our learners, and to get them to reflect. So we used a Fantasy Scenario.

We also used Rewards. In this case they were trophies. Within the town of Northford, which was our virtual town that was on the map you saw earlier, one of the buildings was a museum where the trophy cabinet is located. At the start of the game your trophy cabinet is empty. As you perform certain tasks in the game, for example unlocking different buildings, it unlocks the trophies and those become visible in your trophy cabinet in the museum.

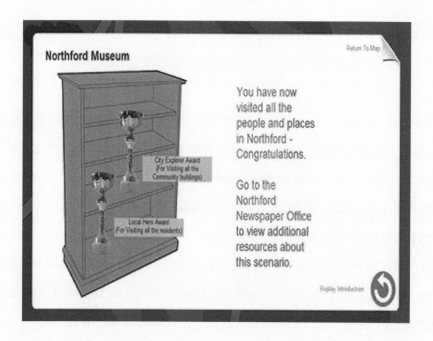

Movement through the game is done according to the learner's actions. Their answers or the way they behave dictate their progress. They're equally unable to move forward until a certain action is completed.

In the next picture there is an example of the hospital at Northford. In the hospital there are objects highlighted in different colors. Visiting the hospital isn't sufficient enough to be able to unlock the hospital and move forward in the game. The learner has to interact with some of the resources within the hospital to achieve that progress.

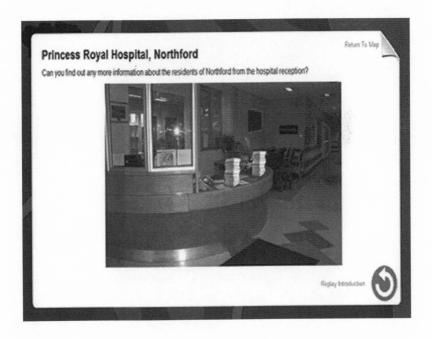

For example, one of the resources is a patient report form which is based on a real one. It gives a bit of background to one of the characters, in this case, our older resident. It gives information on how her behavior might be affected by some of the treatments she's had in the past. So there is a serious message even though it's a game.

Patient Report Form   Northford Hospitals **NHS**
NHS Trust

Discharge Summary

Patient: MacMillan, Joan
Date of Birth: 3 May 1939, Farnborough (Hamps)

Notes:

Joan attended an outpatient appointment having suffered from chronic arthritis in her left hand for approximately 10 years.

While attending the clinic, Joan suffered breathing difficulties brought on by acute anxiety. We brought her in for observation and did not have any cause for further concern.

A referral was made to Northford social services as Joan appeared to be suffering from neglect.

Date: 22 June 2014   Signed: S. Ardman

These are examples of how we introduced Game Mechanics into our E-Learning to create a serious game.

Simon Birt: *Thanks, Richard. Let's talk about the process you went through next. There seem to be a lot of media elements and other resources involved here, and obviously someone has to sit down and design the game out. There are a lot of different levels and it is quite complex. How did you apply all these within your Authoring Tool to achieve your game?*

Richard Price: In these next images next I've actually scanned my original notebook to help illustrate the process.

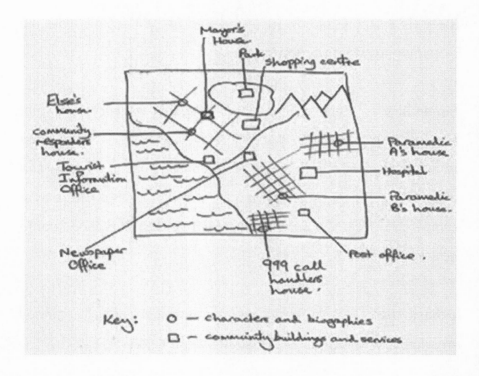

When we were sitting having a planning meeting, right at the beginning, the team and I sat down and we sketched out how our vision of everything would work. So this picture here is the original sketch of the map and how we envisioned how that might look with some of the buildings.

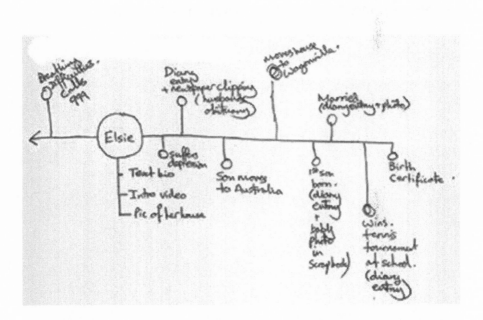

So you get a bit of a back story and a bit of history for the individual characters so we understand why they are the way they are.

The story-boarding for the videos was obviously very important. It's not a mean feat to film anything, especially on this scale.

So, in the Authoring Tool, in terms of the design, we started with a map and then we created a chapter for each character and for each community building. Then we added lots and lots and lots of detail to each of those chapters to make them really rich, so that as the learners encountered them they got lots of information.

And we used an awful lot of variables. I must just emphasize that our Authoring Tool is very good at supporting variables, and we did use an awful lot of them. It depends how comfortable you are with using those. Our Authoring Tool does support them well, but I'm not underestimating the task at hand. And, obviously, lots of testing also well. We think that was very important because, with that many variables, it's easy to make a mistake. So the team very kindly tested this and tested that until they were sick of it!

Simon Birt: *Well, tell us then, the game seems to be well-received from what you've said, and you have explained the type of learners that you had to train. What was the feedback?*

Richard Price: It was aimed at operations staff and paramedics, but we also got some other groups of staff through. The game was generally received very well by the learners and here are some of the comments that we received.

Overall a good tool to remind us of how the patient and others see us.

This Northford video is a good reminder to all YAS staff whether clinical or in support that our approach to others should be with respect.

The course is good and the person sitting at the pc can keep pace.

Provokes opinion which generates discussion.

In the initial pilot, we got about 100 people through in a two-month period. The learning itself took about an hour and a half to work through, so it wasn't a short game. Then there was also additional time to reflect and contribute to the discussion boards I mentioned earlier. And we obviously, at one point, had to present it to the European Commission in Brussels. That was very well-received, and they asked lots of questions and made lots of comments.

Simon Birt: *Okay, and then the final question for this session: How would you view the difficulty of the game creation process versus standard E-Learning content design?*

Richard Price: Well, I'm not going to pretend it was an easy job. It was hard work for everybody involved. But I think if we focus on the similarities to normal E-Learning and how you go about that using Instructional Design, we still have to involve Subject Matter Experts. We still had to script the learning. We still went through the process of identifying our business objectives and looking at the learning outcomes from that.

The differences lay in how we actually presented those learning outcomes and presented them in the gaming environment. It is more challenging to create a game scenario, as it comprised essentially lots of testing as much as anything. And our Authoring Tool is very good at creating linear content but game content was more difficult. It was complex and time-consuming to create the non-linear content that we were asking for. That's where the use of variables and branching comes in. We had a budget of virtually nothing even with the European Union funding. So we had to make use of existing resources and equipment.

All of our actors were members of staff, and the crew was the rest of the team and me. We've never had an experience with this kind of thing before so we were all just working our way through it, learning as we went. We used whatever resources we could. For example, we used an ambulance that wasn't running and was in for some repairs for part of the filming. So, we had to make do with what we had available. Most importantly, though, it was a lot of fun putting all of this together. We enjoyed the authoring process, we enjoyed the actual filming process, and it's been a good experience for all of us. I can recommend it to everybody.

Simon Birt: *I think it's an excellent way to think creatively about how you work with a typical challenge of training for learning outcomes in behavioral change. And to address it with the same technology resources that you use for E-Learning, but with some changes in thinking and creativity, you can address behavioral change through Gaming and Gamification.*

I'd like to thank everybody for joining and thank our guest today, Richard Price, for an excellent presentation on how you use Gamification principles within your E-Learning tool.

Richard Price: Thank you for having me, Simon.

Simon Birt: *You are very welcome. Thank you for being my guest today. Thanks everyone for joining, and happy game creation!*

SIMON BIRT

CHAPTER 9

LEARNING PLANNING

WITH

SIMON BIRT

The session today is about Learning Planning for your job requirements. What do I mean by this? I would like to start off with a definition to set the context for the chapter.

Definition:

Learning Planning is an employee-centric approach for the structuring of personal learning goals. It blends, aligns and records all learning activities to meet the agreed needs of both employer and employee.

There's a lot to consider in that definition. Additionally, it is important to note that Learning Planning is a critical component of employee performance support.

LEARNING PLANNING PROCESS – 4 STEPS

Let's talk about the process of Learning Planning. The best person to create the first draft a Learning Plan is the employee himself or herself. It can be done in conjunction with a line-manager, but the employee really is the best person to start. The Learning Planning approach is actually a 4-step process to get employees to their completed Learning Plan.

STEP ONE - Evaluate the critical requirements of the job.

Listing these critical requirements from the organization's perspective in one column, and then from the employee's perspective in another column may highlight any inconsistencies that would need to be resolved. These can also be aligned by priority, essentially matching the most important areas on both sides.

STEP TWO - Determine key development areas.

The second step determines the employees' key development areas. This makes them think about what it is they want or need to develop, and which missing skills the employer should help to develop. They should consider skills and competencies they currently have, look at development paths to improve and strengthen, and identify entirely new ones that they will need while considering how they might acquire these.

STEP THREE - Select the right learning resources.

The third step is a selection of the right learning resources. Employees have to identify which learning resources are the resources best-suited to their needs. These resources will most likely be located in a mix of places, both online and offline. They may also indicate **relationships** that the employee needs to develop with experts that can help them and networks they can develop. If there are formal qualifications that need to be acquired, they should look into institutions and courses where these are accessible to them and fit their work routine, remembering that much - if not all - of this learning will be done in addition to their jobs.

STEP FOUR – Prioritize.

Prioritize activities into a plan. Employees should involve business partners and colleagues from within their company to help them to do this correctly. Once they have their plans they should discuss them with other colleagues who are going to be affected. Find out what they think, get their feedback, and then prioritize activities in line with organizational goals.

If employees approach their Learning Plans properly, the process should include working with managers to define their key learning activities according to individual needs in the role. First of all, they may need help to analyze their knowledge gaps. They would then need to look at what skills and knowledge they need to acquire, plan their learning resources around that, and align their planning to the organization's goals. If the organization feels comfortable with their learning development plans, they should receive lot of support and help to achieve their goals.

WHY IS LEARNING PLANNING IMPORTANT?

KEY POINT - Many organizations widely recognize the key need for staff to lead and manage change, while simultaneously identifying that employee skills are largely deficient in this area. Furthermore, in managing and developing employee performance in general, the skills of their managers are insufficient.

There are a range of surveys every year indicating that organizations understand the need for managing change, and they also understand that their employees are not necessarily skilled or trained well enough in this area to manage that challenge.

Managers and line-managers are not often well-versed in how to manage and develop employee performance themselves. In recognizing this, it's very important to understand the role that

Learning Planning can play as a tool to help both employees and employers overcome this challenge, and to help close the gap in the skills that are needed to manage and develop employee performance.

LEARNING PLANNING IS CRITICAL TODAY

Learning Planning today is critical to any organization and to the employee for several reasons:

KEY POINT – Managing Learning Resources.
First of all, we have a huge number of readily available resources for learning. For the employee, the challenge is what to learn and from where to get the resources. There may be a wide range of resources available both on the internet and within the intranet of the corporate organization. How does one **focus and structure** what is available to one so that it is effective and helps one to develop?

KEY POINT – We are more responsible for our development than ever before.
We have seen a change in organizational Learning and Development

within the last 10-15 years. In most cases, the ownership of personal career planning has moved from the company to employees, and there are two types of training and development that I would reference here:

1. The more strategic type of training and development which relates to what you would do to prepare for the long term to make sure you are on-track and on-plan for your career goals.

2. The training and development that is needed so you can do your job today, or On-the-Job-Training.

In the first of these, many employers today have significantly reduced their participation as general long-term career development is seen as the employee's responsibility.

Secondly, On-the-Job-Training is at the focus of most of the learning that takes place in organizational Learning and Development. Any soft-skills development such as interpersonal relationship management comes about as a consequence of doing On-The-Job-Training. Soft-skills are developed by the organization only if the employee needs them to get the job done today. If *you* identify that you need soft-skills training, and you do not currently need it for your job, then you will only get that soft-skills training if you take the initiative to learn outside your organization. As more and more employees are at the **center of their development** needs today, this is what happens. This is evidenced by the explosion in MOOCs (Massive Open Online Courses) which have emerged to service the professionals' need to self-develop.

KEY POINT – There are more opportunities for career growth open to the employee.

The world is getting smaller. We can potentially transfer within a company to jobs anywhere in the world more easily, and it's becoming more important that we work to a plan that informs us about how we intend to grow our career paths to include our geographical options. Doing structured planning that helps you identify your goals within a broadly defined framework is no longer bounded by geography or ability to relocate.

KEY POINT – Learning acquisition is a desirable Key Performance Indicator (KPI).

Win the last few years, we have also seen this particular focus on Learning Acquisition as a Key Performance Indicator. Some organizations mandate a set number of hours per month for learning, which is measured and tracked, and then linked to compensation.

KEY POINT – Learning Planning helps you identify your learning gaps, and provides guidance to reach both short and long-term job goals.

It can help you define where you have skill shortages or competencies that are missing, and help you get your job done both in the short-term and then in the longer-term (what you need to do to prepare yourself for that next big step-up in your role or your intended career path).

Within the job that you are working on today (which you are focusing on for the next 12 months to 24 months) and within the larger framework of where your career is going, Learning Planning can provide guidance for you to identify and evaluate your progression and also your requirements.

KEY POINT – Learning Planning helps create a shared learning record with your employer.

If you are doing this planning, you should really be doing it with your line-manager's involvement. If you have business partners within the organization with whom you work, consult them about how you are developing your learning plan. It can not only expose them to what you are planning to do, but also helps you to understand what you should be doing in their eyes, therefore creating what will be an agreed, shared record of learning.

KEY POINT – Learning Planning helps the employees target their needs and align them to their employer's requirements.

For example, if you have the requirement to qualify as a certified accountant or as a certified compliance officer within your organization, there will be a certain amount of testing and learning that you will have to go through. Doing a Learning Plan helps you and your employer decide if that's actually something that's relevant to your current position, or whether you need to move to another role to work in that particular field. Maybe you need to acquire some further skills and competencies first before you attempt to go there. Aligning what the employer would like you to do, or what your employer sees you becoming within the organization, against where you are today is what Learning Planning helps you to do.

CIPD SURVEY

Recently, there was an interesting survey of learning and talent management by the CIPD, which represents about a 130,000 organizational employees, and it states that, " **Only 8% of those companies surveyed that have talent management activities believed the talent activities are very effective."** It also states that, **"11% believe they are fairly or very ineffective."** Those are quite damning statistics coming out of a survey of a large number of organizations in the U.S.A. This survey tells us basically that, although we do a lot of talent management activities, we don't believe that they are effective in getting us where we want to be.

However, all respondents agreed that **"talent management activities targeted the following groups: high potential employees, followed by senior managers and graduates."** So clearly 'the best of the best', as they are viewed by their organizations, are the people that get put forward for talent management development. But where does that leave everyone else?

KEY POINT – Learning Planning increases line-managers' involvement in employee development, and in turn, aids their own development skills.

From the CIPD survey that I mentioned earlier, this is an identified gap in many organizations. Line-managers do not necessarily have enough involvement or the right skill-set to help develop employees correctly. As a manager, it can help you develop performance within your own team. As you go through the organization and become responsible for people, learning how to use Learning Planning for managing your employee's requirements, aspirations and development is a critical part of being a successful manager.

So how does Learning Planning help us get a better picture of all this?

KEY POINT – Learning Planning targets *total* employee development. Mentoring does not.

If you are an organization of 40,000 or 50,000 people, identifying a percentage of that for mentoring may be helpful to your organizational goals, but it isn't inclusive of the general employee base. However, Learning Planning targets *general* employee development. Many organizations have programs for mentoring, or employee fast-track development, which focus on a small number of employees. Far fewer have programs for Learning Planning which can address the entire workforce and have the potential for large impact.

KEY POINT – Learning Planning increases employee satisfaction, involvement and contribution.

If all employees have a Learning Plan, they then feel as though they are on a path to something better than where they currently are. They will respond extremely well to that type of motivation. Increasing employee satisfaction and contribution is critical to maintaining good employee morale.

<u>CHAPTER TEN KEY POINT SUMMARY</u>

<u>LEARNING PLANNING</u>

DEFINITION.

Learning Planning is an employee-centric approach for the structuring of personal learning goals. It blends, aligns and records all learning activities to meet the agreed needs of both employer and employee.

LEARNING PLANNING PROCESS – 4 STEPS.

STEP ONE - Evaluate the critical areas in the job.

STEP TWO - Determine key development areas.

STEP THREE - Select the right learning resources.

STEP FOUR – Prioritize.

WHY IS LEARNING PLANNING IMPORTANT?

1. Learning planning is important because many organizations widely recognize the need to lead and manage change, while simultaneously identifying that employee skills may be deficient in this area.

2. Furthermore, in managing and developing employee performance in general, the skills of their managers are lacking.

216

LEARNING PLANNING IS CRITICAL TODAY.

1. We need to manage our Learning Resources.
2. We are more responsible for our personal development than ever.
3. There are more opportunities for career growth open to the employee.
4. Learning acquisition is a desirable KPI.
5. Learning Planning helps you identify your learning gaps.
6. Learning Planning helps provide guidance to reach job goals.
7. Learning Planning helps retain a shared learning record.
8. Learning Planning helps employees target their needs and align them to the employer's requirements.
9. Learning planning contributes to overcoming the challenges of managing employee performance and development.
10. Learning Planning targets total employee development, not just the top performers.
11. Learning Planning increases employee satisfaction, involvement and contribution.

SIMON BIRT

218

CHAPTER 10

THE ROLE OF

IDEAS AND INNOVATION

IN TRAINING

AT

THE WALT DISNEY CORPORATION

WITH

LEE KITCHEN

In this session Lee often refers to something called the 'Toy Box'. Although he can't share anything that is proprietary to Disney, he has agreed to help out with some links and supporting info that he used to get started. Essentially, Lee took tools that have been available for a while, and designed his own toolbox using them. He then branded this as the 'Toybox' and tailored it to suit the Disney culture. If you are interested in doing a similar type of training approach at your company, you can use ideas such as these to get started.

Lee writes: *"The Toybox workshop is an internal Disney Parks interactive and immersive two-day training experience that focuses on Creative Problem Solving for Innovation and Creativity. It is designed to help teams and individuals get out of their "rivers of thinking" (that day-to-day expertise which may be preventing true innovation) and helps participants tackle challenges from a fresh perspective, using tools (which we call "toys") they have never used before. The process can be applied to an entirely new challenge or simply one that has needed an innovative solution for a while.*

http://www.whatifinnovation.com/

http://www.thinkxic.com/

http://www.prophet.com/home

http://www.ideo.com/

You can learn more about the science of our discipline through schools that offer Masters Programs in CPS and Design Thinking such as Buffalo State University of New York http://creativity.buffalostate.edu/ and the D-School at Stanford http://dschool.stanford.edu."
Lee Kitchen, The Disney Corporation

Here are some examples of the types of methods and tools referred to in this chapter and in the links above:

- Examination of the role and application of innovation

- Approaches to unlocking Creativity

- Design and use of software tool-sets to capture creativity, problem-solving, ideation, work-flow and process

- Model for Productive Thinking and Ideation (see below)[3]

---

3   The ThinkX Productive Thinking model is a six-step problem-solving and opportunity-finding methodology that builds on 50 years of research by the Creative Education Foundation, 30 years of research by NASA, and five years of field testing. It combines the situation analyses and ideation strengths of CEF's methodology with the success criteria and project mapping techniques of NASA's iDEF methodology. Attribution for this image and text ~ *http://www.thinkxic.com/*

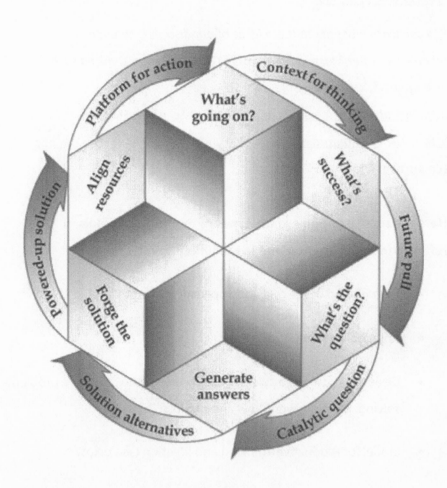

Image of the ThinkX six-step Productive Thinking Model

Simon Birt: *Good morning, everyone, and welcome to today's conversation about the role of Innovation and Ideas in Training. This is your host, Simon Birt. My guest today is Lee Kitchen who is joining us from the Walt Disney Corporation.*

Lee Kitchen in the Disney ID8 Lounge

As I start out, I want to put some context in place for today's presentation.

IDEAS AND INNOVATION CONTEXT

Learning Transformation, something that we're all involved in, comes partly through using good ideas in innovation and creativity to deliver engaging learning activities that result in better employee performance.

That's where we're trying to go when we're thinking about ways of creating environments and simulations that help train employees to change behavior, or to do things differently from the way they do it today.

When I was thinking about who I would have on this session, Lee was the perfect person that came to mind because he lives and breathes this for Disney, flying all over the world and training employees. I'll follow my usual format of asking eight questions of Lee to explain a little more about what he does, so that it helps us all to understand and appreciate the challenges, and also the successes, that he has in his job.

Simon Birt: *So Lee, let's start with Question One which is an easy one to start with: Could you please describe, in your words, what you do at Disney?*

Lee Kitchen: Yes, I can. This is really cool and looks awesome on a business card; I am a Creative Problem-Solving Expert. And yes, it is a discipline! I actually help people on a daily basis. I help them come up with ideas, and I work for a small but mighty team of people that are part of the Parks and Resorts Marketing Team. So these are the people that are responsible for telling everybody in the world about all of our parks: Disneyland, Walt Disney World, Disneyland Paris, Hong Kong Disneyland, Tokyo Disneyland, and the soon-to-be Shanghai Disneyland. I help those people come up with ideas, and basically we're a team called 'Creator Bank'. It's, again, a small group that helps a lot of different business units around the Walt Disney Company specifically in Parks and Resorts.

We do three specific things:

1. Inspiring: We are responsible for creating a culture of innovation, so we're responsible for inspiring everybody, and we do a lot of different things to do that. We help create

collaborative work spaces, places that people can go to get out of their offices, to get inspiration, to host Ideation sessions, etc. We host a monthly forum to showcase trends and things that have inspired people throughout the months. We invite people both here at Disney World and in Anaheim at Disneyland to inspire them.

2. Inventing: The next thing we do is called 'Inventing', and Inventing is taking our teams through a process structure of creativity and different thinking; to be able to get them from the start of their project to the end of their project, and all the time being more collaborative and thinking differently. We use a process that we call the 'Toybox', which I'll say a little more about as we get into it, to help them do that.

3. Instructing: And then finally, our third 'I' and that is Instructing. We actually host a two-day training class that we call the 'Toybox' which is a method by which we help people understand their challenges; to help people use the data about their consumers and to get inspired by that data to help generate ideas. We help people learn how to think laterally and think differently about when they create ideas

for their challenges, and then we also help people refine those ideas and help them make selections.

So three I's: Inspiring, Inventing, and Instructing.

Simon Birt: *Okay, and they're all themed within the Toybox that you've created as a set of tools?*

Image of the Disney Toybox Training Manual

Lee Kitchen: Yes.

Simon Birt: *Would you use the set of tools in the Toybox all the time or do you select which ones you need for a particular project?*

Lee Kitchen: It really depends. We have projects both big and small, and one of the cool things about our Toybox process is that it's totally scale-able. As we teach it, we basically let our participants know that they can use it just on a small project when they need a little bit of different thinking. They can use it for a full project such as a full three or four month project where the result they want is something drastically different than what they had before. It's just a creative problem-solving process that can help any challenge that you're working on.

Simon Birt: *Okay. So talk to us a little bit here about how you use ideas and creativity, and then how that leads to innovation in your employee training. Can you give some insight to that?*

Lee Kitchen: As I think of this question, one of the things that Toybox training does a lot is bring people together in a collaborative way, and then it also helps dispel those myths about how "certain people are creative and certain people aren't." In many organizations, some people have 'Creativity' in their title. And much of the culture thinks, "Oh, wait a minute. Those are the people that do creative. I don't come up with ideas. Those are the people who come up with ideas." What we try to teach in our Toybox training is that it's all of our responsibility to do that. We're going to teach a method, and we hope you'll make it a habit in your day-to-day working life to be able to think differently about what you're doing.

The other myth we try to dispel is the 'Creativity-in-a-Box idea'. So right now, many people use creativity. They pull it off their shelves. But they don't really use creativity unless somebody says, "Okay, we need a big idea for the next week's campaign. Go in that room and sit there for an hour and come out [with good ideas]." And then we pull Creativity out of the box. We open it up. We sing and dance with Creativity, and then we put it back in the box when we're done. What we're trying to impart, however, post-taking this class, is that Creativity should be part of our day-to-day life. We should be thinking differently about each step. Just because you work in Finance, Pricing or Legal doesn't mean you can't use creativity to solve your challenges.

Simon Birt: *Can you share with us the types of training sessions that you hold and how they're received by your employees?*

Lee Kitchen: Again, we use the Toybox. The Toybox is basically a couple of different things. One is the structure and place; a structured process to be able to always think differently through each depth of the process. Number Two is a set of behaviors. So we say that you can have the best process and structure in place, but if people aren't behaving helpfully to support that structure, then it's all for nothing. We say "behaviors eat process for breakfast."

We keep nine different creativity behaviors that support the learning that we do, and then I teach a series of tools that we actually call 'Toys.' When we started it, we wanted to call it the 'Toybox' on purpose because we wanted people to have permission to have more fun at work. One of the behaviors that we talked about in Toy Box is Playfulness, and Playfulness is all about not taking ourselves too seriously. It's about having a little bit of the lighter touch. There's brain science behind [how you behave] when you are relaxed, you know. We always ask people, "Where do you come up with your best ideas?" and they always say, "the shower, driving to work, walking the dog." Nobody ever said, "It's at work," right?

Simon Birt: *Yes. Exactly.*

Lee Kitchen: So, to us, there's a reason behind that. When you're at work, your brain is in work-mode and you can't really open yourself up consciously to get at all that great creativity that you have stored in there. If you have just a little bit of a lighter touch, it actually helps you open up the special doorway in your brain to allow that creativity out. So it's a two-day learning course. We actually extract people from the organization [to do it]. The Toybox is a kind of a holistic approach from start to finish. We start with a phase called 'Vision', which is about collaborating to define what we're solving for. So many times when you get a project, you're just basically on-the-go. "You guys go solve this [one particular] challenge," but nobody really challenges that [request]. Why are we doing that? Why are we doing it now? What does success mean? What's the context behind it? So we have a collaborative approach to make sure that everybody is grounded on the information, and that everybody in the team is allowed to ask a lot of questions about it. So they're all grounded and they all feel like we're solving for the right challenge [together].

You don't want to get a month down the road and realize, "Oh, no! We're totally solving for the wrong thing." I'm sure that's happened to some of you before. You're probably nodding your heads out there in virtual land. And then also we teach them how to use the data. We have all this great consumer data, and we teach them how to use that data to be inspired with great ideas that are really consumer-centric. Not only do we just use the data, we actually go out into the world to be inspired. We get a team of people, and we go out and talk to our consumers face-to-face. We go out and we engage with experts on our challenge. It's a lot more inspiring for people to come up with the ideas. We spend a lot of time creating ideas. It's a big phase in the middle where we create ideas, and then after that, we spend time refining, analyzing, and selecting those ideas, after which we move them forward for execution.

Simon Birt: *It sounds to me as if it's like a lot of experimentation, a lot of trial, some error, and then you come up with what works best. Now, how do you find that this applies when you're trying to break down barriers with employees, and then between employees and managers, in the same session?*

Lee Kitchen: It's really great, actually, because we mix up the groups. I mean, just within our marketing and sales teams we create small, intimate classes of about sixteen to twenty people. We find that people recognize each other in the workplace because they see them in the elevator, but no one stops and talks to that person, right?

So we find that we get a more collaborative approach because we've got people mingling from different departments that never mingled before. This is also why we created the open collaboration space, because you might be standing in the line for Starbucks talking, and realize that the person behind you is solving for a similar challenge. Then you meet up and you talk about it, and you help each other through the challenge collaboratively. It's one of those unwritten things about Toybox training. Getting to know everyone, and then those people see each other again when we invite them to our 'Creative Couch', which is our monthly inspiration meeting. So it's a pretty cool transitional lunch.

Simon Birt: *Although you're a very big organization, it sounds as if all of these sessions are conducted among a small number of employees at a time. Is that correct?*

Lee Kitchen: Yes. That's correct.

Simon Birt: *So it could apply that this type of interaction training, or session, could work with smaller companies as well. They wouldn't necessarily have to apply just to big companies?*

Lee Kitchen: Oh, definitely. Definitely. Yes.

Simon Birt: *Okay.*

Lee Kitchen: And, actually, there are a couple of methods that we teach which are specifically about creating ideas. We call one the 'Big Brain Storm', where you get one person in front of the room and twenty people shouting out ideas. We actually had to change that and say, "Look at what we do here when we do that [in big groups], but then let's break up into smaller teams of three or four," and all of a sudden, it becomes this conversational idea creation as if it were in your living room or your local bar or whatever. It makes people more comfortable, and the quality of output from just changing that dynamic is different. It's just so great.

Simon Birt: *It sounds fantastic, and you've obviously been doing this for a while. So tell us a little bit about some of the successes and failures of what you've seen in this type of approach to training.*

Lee Kitchen: Okay. We started in early 2012. We've trained over 1700 Disney Marketing and Sales employees, and one of the things that we really tried to instill in the participants about the Toybox is that it's very portable, and it's very easily usable the moment that they walk out [of the training]. So many times you might take training classes or go to seminars or conferences, and when you get back on the Monday after the conference people ask, "Hey, how was the conference?" Either you don't remember all the details, or you don't really feel you know how to put that content into practice. With the Toybox, though, they can walk out of the room, and they can use it to select their vacation. They can use it the next day to help decide where they go to lunch, you know. It's so portable. They can use it on something small. They can change the way that they do a normal meeting. What we try to instill in people is this: if you don't use one of these Toys at least within a week after leaving here, you may not use it ever again. And so what happens is we get a lot of feedback the very next week after our Toybox training. "Hey, I'm about ready to switch up and do an energizer at my meeting. Can you give me a suggestion for that?" And so we do a lot of consultation. When they're setting up a facilitation, someone might say "Hey, I'm with Industrial Engineering, and we're thinking about this challenge, and we're going to use this particular Toy. This is how I'm going to set it up." And we help them through solving that challenge. We find that the ones that contact us a lot for consultation obviously took the content and used it.

Simon Birt: *And the others?*

Lee Kitchen: The ones we never hear from again, they most likely went right back to the same way that they did things. This is unfortunate because, again, this is applicable in whatever business that you're working on. But, I would say of the 1700 people that I've consulted with, at least 600 of those people are actually using it. And they're spilling over into the other parts of the organization, too. So, I'm feeling pretty confident that we've definitely changed the culture with how people approach this. Plus, I go to the meetings myself where they're using the content, and it's amazing to watch because they've taken it to a whole new level. Not only did their leadership people give them permission to do that, but they've actually found success, and it's just by changing their meetings. Here's a great example: One person from our Brand and Strategy Team has the same meeting every couple of weeks called the 'Integrated Communication Plan Meeting'. And one of the things we teach and talk about is called 'rewording', which is basically changing the names of things to inspire an internal theme. It's a super-easy thing to do, right? They changed the name of that meeting to 'Favorite Meeting'. Now they have spill-over attendance of this meeting and people actually consider it their favorite meeting. All they did was just change the word for it. It was just a simple change that made a huge difference. The tools and Toys that we teach are a pretty common sense approach. Just something as small as that made a big difference.

Simon Birt: *I'm guessing also that once employees feel empowered to use creativity, this is when you see these iterations of what you've taught starting to blossom. Is that correct or not?*

Lee Kitchen: That is correct and that's actually the joy of what I do. Because I've been at Disney for 29 years, I've seen it all. I've seen everything come and go, and it's amazing for me to see this culture change. It actually comes back to me and helps me with my own job because when I host sessions where I'm asking these people for ideas, now that they're skilled-up and trained-up, the output of the brainstorm sessions is of so much higher quality than it used to be even three years ago. The improvement definitely shows and it helps me with my own day-to-day, which is also great.

Simon Birt: *Yes. Every trainer loves to get reinforcement feedback, to know that what they've taught is actually being embraced rather than just listened to. We're all interested and driven by business value these days, and as you know, sometimes business value is easy to see in the type of training that you're running and sometimes it's not. I suspect with this type of training it can be quite hard sometimes to demonstrate your business value and key benefits. So could you tell us more about how you go about doing this, and how you manage to prove to your stakeholders that what you do really does impact the business?*

Lee Kitchen: Yes. That's one of the things that we try to drive home, especially when a whole team of folks say, "Hey, we want to take this creativity training because we're ready to do something." So we really promote heavily. For example, the whole entire Promotion Team wants to think differently about the way they do business. So how we'd challenge them would be like this: We'd say, "Okay. You guys come in and be Toy Box trained. But don't just be trained and go off and forget about it. Plan a project that you need to think differently about, and take all of those people that you trained, and have them collaborate. Work together on that project from start to finish." This way, not only does it bring to life the things that we taught them, but it gives them an immediate way to use the content that we train them in, and have it affect their bottom line and their business. And then we coach them through it. We either try to coach them, or we were on the teams ourselves to help them through those projects. I've probably hosted, or been a part of, about twenty projects since we started this training, big projects that at the end we came up with something totally different than what we've done in years past.

Simon Birt: *Do they ever write back to you later on and say, "I picked this up in your Toybox session, I used it on this project, and it was really successful?" Do you get that feedback afterwards?*

Lee Kitchen: We do. It's nice to see, and a lot of times people are so busy they might not take the time to leave feedback. But when they do, it's pretty remarkable. There's a real-time example where I trained a group of people in Operations over at one of our parks where there were a lot of rule changes. I extracted them from the organization, then I taught them how to use the Toy Box. I taught them how to think differently about what they would do. Within six months they came up with a plan, they invited me back over, and they walked me through it. They had measured what some Cast Members were doing, basically to keep their Cast Members excited because there are a lot of changes going on with this one park. I come from an Operations background, and the ideas that they came up with were so different from anything I'd ever seen before. It was just so cool to see. Not only that, but all of them were equally excited about it.

One of the great things about this process is that it takes the entire team through from start to finish. When you collaborate on a project from start to finish, you don't get a moment when you are in the middle of a project and you invite in the other people that are actually going to execute it for you, and they say, "Wait a minute. These ideas won't work. I wasn't a part of this idea." So now everybody's equally passionate because they have all defined the vision. They all went on and got inspired by their consumer, or by their end-user. They all created the idea together. They all refined the idea, and they're all going to be the ones to execute the idea, so they're super excited to see it happen. So it's an amazing thing when it works like that. It's really great.

Simon Birt: *We've talked a lot in this session about the Toybox. How did you start to look at the Toybox and the problem-solving tools that that you use? How would one start a program with this type of* *training approach? Can you give us some insight into how you got started, and where you would start if you were doing this today?*

Lee Kitchen: Yes. I think that one of the key factors in embracing it was getting leadership buy-in at the very start of it. One of the things we did was to spend three months talking to all of our senior leaders and basically asking, " What is it that's preventing you from being creative and innovative?" And, not surprisingly, their top points were, "We can't be more creative because we're always in what we call 'ER mode'. We're always rushing to the next problem."

There's no formal structure to getting ideas. They get stuck in the organization. "Do I send it to my leader? Do I send it to my senior leader? I don't even know how to have an idea." So that was a challenge.

Another thing that they talked about was the lack of collaboration because we were a 'relay team'. There is a team of people that said "We decide the strategy and we pass it off to the people who look at the consumers, and then they pass it off to the people with creative ideas, and then they pass it off to the people who execute the ideas," and there was really no collaboration in that. So we actually had them help us design and customize the course. And then, we taught them first. All of our senior leaders, and all of our senior vice presidents and vice presidents, were the first people to go to this class so that we could get their buy-in to lead that charge. Basically, we worked from the top down. But, as we started with our manager and associate level employees, we tasked them like a grassroots movement. There are some people that may not be trained so they're going to have to be brave. They have to be courageous because people don't always like change. It's going to be challenging. And you're going to get that crooked look on people's faces like, "Why are we doing this differently?" But we want them to keep going.

"Come on! We're going to do this differently?" "No! I don't want that." That's where the top-down approach is important, then basically empowering the people that came to the class to make it a grassroots movement. That's pretty great. We actually give them a prize at the end of the training. It's a deck of cards that have all the different Toys as a quick reference. We ask them to put the card that has the logo 'Toybox' on it, which uses the Toy Story content, at the front. We've got great content such as pictures of Woody and Buzz, and we have them put these on the outside of their offices so that everybody knows they share the same language. One of the cool things about Toybox is that it gives us this communal language that we can all understand together. So, even if you work in Legal, or you work in Promotions, or you work in Merchandising, you can say, "You know what green housing is? Cool! Let's create some ideas." We're being expansionists. It's fun seeing everybody use the lingo and understand each other equally.

Simon Birt: *But I can imagine some people listening here are probably thinking "Well, I understand how that works in Disney. Come on. Toy Box and everything else - that's obvious. But my company's way more serious than that. We don't work in entertainment. We work in insurance, for example." How do we have something that fits there?*

Lee Kitchen: I challenge those folks too. Just because we have a mouse and a train and a monorail, doesn't mean that you can't do this. I've read so many articles about small companies either empowering their employees or teaching them creativity. I just read one about a Jamaican restaurant that specializes in Jamaican Jerk Chicken that allowed their employees to help create ideas and then also help refine them. This is a small restaurant chain in Jamaica that used Playfulness and Fun and Freshness to instill in their organization and employees a sense of pride. So I say it can be done anywhere. Having fun and being playful, you don't necessarily have to have characters to do that.

It's changing the name of a meeting. I mean, I know this thing is really simple, but it makes all the difference. We also do energizers at the beginning of our meetings. Instead of just jumping right to the content, we stand people up. We have them introduce themselves to each other and then tell stories about something. It gets people laughing and playful, and it ends up making the meeting more productive. It's as simple as that. A lot of people will show a funny YouTube video to start a meeting.

Even if the content is serious, you can still make it fun and playful. Giving people that common language is pretty essential because everybody is on common ground. I just have to tell this story: We use a fake challenge when we do Toy Box training, and we read the challenge up front and it's full of initialisms and acronyms. And I ask, "How many people have ever gotten a strategic or creative read that looks like this, and you're in a meeting and you don't want to raise your hand because you don't understand any of what they're saying?" And everybody raises their hands. It's so hilarious because -

especially at Disney - we have lists of acronyms. We tell people, "If you're going to inspire people to work on a challenge, write it so everybody understands it. Take out the initialisms. Make it compelling and inspiring. Instead of saying, "How might we make more money?", how about saying, "How might we make our consumers so excited they can't wait to come here and have so much fun with their family?" We just changed the wording of our challenges and, again, it's a simple change but it makes a huge difference.

Simon Birt: *This leads on really to the next question. How do you follow up afterwards, and keep that passion and enthusiasm going that you bring to the sessions?*

Lee Kitchen: We do a couple of different things. For example, once a month, we do 'Creative Couch'. Creative Couch is the place where everybody can come and get inspired. One of the behaviors that we instill in people is called 'Fresher', and it's basically always making sure that we get a fresh perspective on the things that we're doing: drive a different way to work, read a different magazine, talk to somebody that you've never talked to before. Wherever you go, get inspiration from it. When people ask you for ideas, you can make connections. We invite all the people we've trained to Creative Couch. They automatically put it on their calendars to come. We also invite them to an online area called 'Creative Lab', which is like a Pinterest for work. The idea is that if someone sees something cool out there, whether they're just surfing the internet, or see a billboard, or whatever it may be, post it up here so we can all talk about it and all be inspired by it. We ask them to just spend ten minutes looking at the content for inspiration. Our senior leaders do it. I say, "If our SVP can sit there and look at ten minutes of awesome YouTube videos, you can too." It's just taking time to separate yourself from your project, get inspiration, and then go back to the super-important things to do. We also host 'Lunch and Learns'. We'll take one specific Toy and will actually ask one of the participants, "Hey, do you have a small challenge? Won't you bring that in and we'll practice the Toy on your challenge?"

Simon Birt: *Tell us about the future plans. I'm really excited about the Creative Lab, and the idea of using virtual social connections within the company to further training or follow-up training. Tell us about the more about this.*

Lee Kitchen: The Creative Lab is basically a virtual social site that people can go to, and if they have seen something inspiring, they can post it. It's a structured way for people to submit ideas for the organization. It's also a place where we crowd-source ideas. If somebody has a challenge that they want to post, they can crowd-source it. Here's another tip that I'll give you : One of the ways to make your Ideation sessions more magical is to invite people that are not close to the project. We find that when you mix up people that are experts with what we call 'unbiased ideas', which are ideas from those people that just love creating ideas but they have nothing to do with your business at all, that's when the Ideation magic happens, and that's why Creative Lab is really great. We not only have Marketing and Sales Cast Members. We have Cast Members from Operations and from other Business Units such as ESPN, ABC, and Marvel that are mixing together with us. It's amazing because they know nothing about the challenge, so they're not thinking about it in the same way that everybody else is. They throw in something that inspires the experts and the quality of the ideas that we get is excellent. We're actually taking our Toybox process to our Creative Lab to help create a virtual space where people can learn more about it. They can practice it without being embarrassed. We're actually giving them a persona so they don't even have to put their real names on it, and they can just have a little fun learning how to do it. Plus, there's also a discussion board on how people use the different Toys. As we're moderating it, we'll chime in and show how we've used the Toys compared to what they've done.

Simon Birt: *We've had a lot of great ideas and content from getting started, creating the Toy Box, and then moving on to using tools for creating level playing fields where people can feel empowered to bring ideas and creativity to the process. How you follow up is also enlightening. All of this is very important to creating business value in training.*

Thank you, Lee, for sharing your knowledge and your experience with us. To everyone else, enjoy your training wherever you're doing it, whatever you're working on.

Lee Kitchen: Thank you. It's been fun!

Simon Birt: *Yes, it has. Happy creating, learning and training everyone!*

LEARNING UNSCRIPTED

SIMON BIRT

ACKNOWLEDGEMENTS

I cannot say enough about my fantastic interviewees: Charles Jennings, Karel Geeraert, Marvin Mullins, Richard Price and Lee Kitchen. I wish that this book could properly convey the enthusiasm and character of these thought-leaders, and it has been a privilege to have access to their insights and comments (and they are exceedingly nice people).

My grateful thanks to my wife, who has great ideas and helps me to shape my own. Without her encouragement and belief, I would never be able to achieve what I do. I am often in her debt and constantly amazed at my good fortune.

My sincere gratitude goes to two long-term colleagues and friends, Scott Sloan and Charles Beech (gentlemen with whom I would happily work, visit a maritime museum, or go on a photography expedition), for their support, wisdom, and guidance throughout the recent years.

Thanks also to my parents, who understood the value of a good education and ensured I received it, despite my best efforts to do otherwise. Consequently, I have been edified in my adult life with extraordinary opportunities to learn and share the tools and knowledge of the 21st century with others.

To Stan McDougall and Linda Ellison, the parents of my gorgeous, fun, hard-working and all-round fabulous wife, my sincerest appreciation! I couldn't ask for kinder and more supportive in-laws.

To my wonderful, precocious and beautiful daughter, Isabella, who reminds me daily how much the next generation will rely heavily upon technology, online information, virtual reality and gaming...and, that I should stop pestering her to put down her phone and go outside for exercise and fresh air!

Lastly, a giant 'thank you' to all other friends, family and colleagues who have given me their best wishes and encouragement. For me, my work is a pleasure, and I am delighted to finally share this with you.

Happy Learning ~ Simon

Printed in Great Britain
by Amazon.co.uk, Ltd.,
Marston Gate.